a cup of
Living
Water

for a joyful soul

By David R. Veerman

TYNDALE HOUSE PUBLISHERS, INC.
WHEATON, ILLINOIS

Visit Tyndale's exciting Web site at www.tyndale.com

A Cup of Living Water for a Joyful Soul copyright © 2001 by Tyndale House Publishers. All rights reserved.

Cover photograph copyright © 2001 by Kazutomo Kawai/Photonica. All rights reserved.

Material written and compiled by The Livingstone Corporation, Carol Stream, IL, and the following individuals: Katherine Cloyd, indexer, and Joan Guest, editor.

Scripture quotations are taken from the *Holy Bible,* New Living Translation, copyright © 1996. Used by permission of Tyndale House Publishers, Inc., Wheaton, Illinois 60189. All rights reserved.

New Living Translation and the New Living Translation logo are registered trademarks of Tyndale House Publishers, Inc.

ISBN 0-8423-5562-6

Printed in the United States of America

03 02 01
5   4   3   2   1

Contents

Introduction

Cups of living water come in two forms: those given and those received. Jesus himself made that point when he said, "If you give even a cup of cold water to one of the least of my followers, you will surely be rewarded" (Matthew 10:42). He also remarked, "If anyone gives you even a cup of water because you belong to the Messiah, I assure you, that person will be rewarded" (Mark 9:41). Following Jesus includes giving cups of water to those in need as well as accepting cups of water from others when we are in need. And ultimately, living water has only one source: Jesus Christ.

Living Water

So, what is living water? When Jesus used that term in a conversation with a hurting woman (John 4:4-26), he wasn't inventing a new concept (Proverbs 18:4; Isaiah 58:11; Ezekiel 47:1-12). The Old Testament prophet Jeremiah recorded the expression twice. First, God described himself this way: "My people have done two evil things: They have forsaken me—the fountain of living water. And they have dug for themselves cracked cisterns that can hold no water at all!" (Jeremiah 2:13). Later, Jeremiah used the phrase in a prayer:

"O Lord, the hope of Israel, all who turn away from you will be disgraced and shamed. They will be buried in a dry and dusty grave, for they have forsaken the Lord, the fountain of living water" (Jeremiah 17:13).

Centuries later, Jesus began his conversation with the woman at the well with a request. He asked her for a drink. The Lord of the universe placed himself in debt to a sinful, outcast woman. He honored and shocked her by addressing her in the first place and by asking for her help. What a novel concept! Jesus disarmed her defenses against his help by seeking her help.

The woman's curiosity overcame her reserve and pain. She began to ask him questions: "Why are you asking me for a drink?" and "Where would you get this living water?" Eventually, she was able to receive living water from Jesus, the "man who told me everything I ever did!" (John 4:29). The living water is the living Word, and it does have an uncanny way of telling us everything we ever did. It also tells us everything that has been done for us!

Not long after that episode in Samaria, Jesus announced to the crowds in Jerusalem that he was the source of living water for them. "If you are thirsty, come to me! If you believe in me, come and drink! For the Scriptures declare that rivers of living water will flow out from within" (John 7:37-38). John explains that Jesus was speaking of the Holy Spirit, who would be given to those who believe (John 7:39).

Are You a Joyful Soul?

While it can certainly be said that love is the fore-
most external characteristic of genuine followers
of Jesus Christ (John 13:34-35), one of the clearest
internal characteristics of Jesus' disciples is joy. Joy
immediately follows love in the list of attributes (or
fruit) of the Spirit-led life found in Galatians 5:22.
In his high priestly prayer for all who would come
to believe in him (John 17:1-26), Jesus specifically
identified joy as the purpose of his ministry. He
also connected joy with the Word: "I have told them
many things while I was with them so they would be
filled with my joy. I have given them your word"
(John 17:13-14). If you have Christ, you have joy. Let
it flow.

The birth, care, and feeding of a joyful soul begin
and continue with Jesus and his Word. If you desire
to grow and to preserve your joy, you must continually rely on God's input through his Word. The
living water that flows out of you will be the living
water that flows into you.

How to Use These Cups and Sips of Living Water

The cups of living water in these pages represent
both forms of living water: some for you to receive
and some for you to pass on after you receive. Take
time to reflect after each reading. Consider what
God is offering you in each soul-satisfying drink of
his living water. Then ask him to direct you to

someone else who might find help from those same words. And don't forget the pattern Jesus sometimes used—helping others by asking for their help.

Drink deeply and continuously from our source of living water, the Holy Spirit, who lives in all those who believe in Jesus Christ.

a cup of . . .

Access to God

LIVING WATER

Keep on asking, and you will be given what you ask for. Keep on looking, and you will find. Keep on knocking, and the door will be opened.

MATTHEW 7:7

Let us come boldly to the throne of our gracious God. There we will receive his mercy, and we will find grace to help us when we need it.

HEBREWS 4:16

We can be confident that he will listen to us whenever we ask him for anything in line with his will. And if we know he is listening when we make our requests, we can be sure that he will give us what we ask for.

1 JOHN 5:14-15

Thirst-quenching thought for the day

God hears us when we pray because we belong to him. As his children, we can confidently approach our loving Father with any confession, concern, problem, or request. God is never too busy to listen and never too preoccupied to pay attention. If what we ask for is what God knows is best for us, he will give it to us. Asking "according to his will" means wanting what *he* wants us to have, not demanding what we want regardless of the consequences.

Don't be intimidated by God. Approach him with reverence, with respect, and with *confidence,* knowing that he will listen carefully to whatever you (his child) ask and that he will give you what is truly best.

Sip to take away
When was the last time you presented God with a bold request?

a cup of . . .

Adoption by God

LIVING WATER

His Holy Spirit speaks to us deep in our hearts and tells us that we are God's children.

ROMANS 8:16

See how very much our heavenly Father loves us, for he allows us to be called his children, and we really are! But the people who belong to this world don't know God, so they don't understand that we are his children. Yes, dear friends, we are already God's children, and we can't even imagine what we will be like when Christ returns. But we do know that when he comes we will be like him, for we will see him as he really is.

1 JOHN 3:1-2

Thirst-quenching
thought for the day

We can call ourselves children of God! Through the work of Christ and our faith in him, we have been born again and adopted into God's family. No wonder the world does not know us—we've changed!

If God has chosen to make us his children now, just think of what he will do for us in the future! Through John, God says that we will be like Christ, fully bearing the family likeness.

What love!

What a life!

What a plan!

What a future!

Sip to take away

Regardless of what the world thinks, you are special. Regardless of your status in society, you are a member of God's family. Regardless of pessimistic predictions, your future is bright. Christ has made you a child of God.

a cup of . . .

Alertness

LIVING WATER

Stay awake and be prepared, because you do not know the day or hour of my return.

MATTHEW 25:13

Since you don't know when they will happen, stay alert and keep watch.

MARK 13:33

Devote yourselves to prayer with an alert mind and a thankful heart.

COLOSSIANS 4:2

Thirst-quenching thought for the day

Before leaving his disciples, Jesus promised that he would return. And he told them that like his first coming, his second coming would be a surprise—no one would know the day or hour. They were to be alert, prepared, and ready. How do you stay alert?

Months of planning go into a wedding, the birth of a baby, a career change, the purchase of a home, or a business venture. How much more should we prepare for Christ's return? It's the most important event of our lives, and its results will last for eternity.

Preparing for Christ's return does not mean selling everything you own and moving to the top of a mountain to look for him in the air. No one knows when he will come back, and he has work for us to do in the meantime. Getting prepared means studying God's Word and living for Christ every day. It means recognizing the urgency of telling others about Christ.

Sip to take away

Are you prepared? Are you ready? Christ is coming back. Be alert! Praise the Lord!

a cup of . . .

Anticipation

LIVING WATER

Come, let us sing to the Lord! Let us give a joyous shout to the rock of our salvation!

PSALM 95:1

Enter his gates with thanksgiving; go into his courts with praise. Give thanks to him and bless his name. For the Lord is good. His unfailing love continues forever, and his faithfulness continues to each generation.

PSALM 100:4-5

I was glad when they said to me, "Let us go to the house of the Lord."

PSALM 122:1

Thirst-quenching thought for the day

Some call it "the Sabbath blues." After a late Saturday night, Sunday morning comes too early, and the prospect of getting up, dressing up, and showing up for church seems very unappealing. Yet we often drag ourselves (and our families) there and *force* ourselves to go through the motions of worship. According to these psalms, however, church services should be occasions of joy where we fill the air with thankful praise. We should have a sense of anticipation as we prepare to gather in God's presence.

This positive, joyful attitude comes from realizing that God is good, that his love is deep, strong, and personal, and that he is faithful and true. Understanding that God loves us, remembering what he has done for us, and knowing that we are his people should make us want to shout and sing with joy. What a great God we have!

Sip to take away

Next Sunday, approach worship with thanksgiving and praise. Take time on Saturday to anticipate meeting with other believers.

a cup of . . .

Anxiety-Free Living

LIVING WATER

*I tell you, don't worry about everyday life—whether
you have enough food, drink, and clothes. Doesn't
life consist of more than food and clothing? Look at
the birds. They don't need to plant or harvest or put
food in barns because your heavenly Father feeds
them. And you are far more valuable to him than
they are. Can all your worries add a single moment
to your life? Of course not.*   MATTHEW 6:25-27

*Don't worry about anything; instead, pray about
everything. Tell God what you need, and thank him
for all he has done. If you do this, you will experience God's peace, which is far more wonderful than
the human mind can understand. His peace will
guard your hearts and minds as you live in Christ
Jesus.*   PHILIPPIANS 4:6-7

Thirst-quenching
thought for the day

Life is filled with opportunities to worry . . . at home, at school, on the job. In fact, it's possible to be anxious about everything. Here Paul presents the antidote to anxiety—prayer. Realizing that God is in control, that he loves us, and that Christ is making intercession for us should turn our worries into prayers. This means talking to God about *everything* and turning every concern, decision, and relationship over to him. We will feel anxiety melt away as we lean on our loving Lord. And we will know his peace.

God's peace is not found through positive thinking, conflict resolution, or emotional release. It comes from knowing God and from trusting him. It reaches into the very depths of our being.

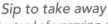

Sip to take away
Instead of worrying, pray and experience God's peace, which is "far more wonderful than the human mind can understand."

a cup of...

Assurance

LIVING WATER

Go and make disciples of all the nations, baptizing them in the name of the Father and the Son and the Holy Spirit. Teach these new disciples to obey all the commands I have given you. And be sure of this: I am with you always, even to the end of the age.

MATTHEW 28:19-20

With my authority, take this message of repentance to all the nations, beginning in Jerusalem: "There is forgiveness of sins for all who turn to me."

LUKE 24:47

Thirst-quenching thought for the day

"I'm afraid, Dad. I don't want to go!"

"Don't worry, son. I'll be with you."

"Mommy! Mommy! I had a terrible dream."

"I'm right here, honey. It's okay. You'll be fine."

Remember being encouraged or comforted as a child? Just the assurance of a loved one's presence made everything all right.

Now you are all grown-up, an adult. But you still get scared and still have anxious nightmares about the future, your finances, and your family. You long for the assurance of a strong hand and loving word. You feel burdened and alone.

But you're not alone. God is there. The promise ("I am with you always.") Jesus gave his disciples as he sent them into the world is also for you!

Sip to take away

Whatever your feelings or doubts, Jesus is with you. Trust him! Take heart! Have hope! Be encouraged! Move out in faith!

a cup of . . .

Attitude

LIVING WATER

Your heavenly Father already knows all your needs, and he will give you all you need from day to day if you live for him and make the Kingdom of God your primary concern.   MATTHEW 6:32-33

Since you have been raised to new life with Christ, set your sights on the realities of heaven, where Christ sits at God's right hand in the place of honor and power. Let heaven fill your thoughts. Do not think only about things down here on earth. For you died when Christ died, and your real life is hidden with Christ in God.   COLOSSIANS 3:1-3

Thirst-quenching thought for the day

The world's offers of security, happiness, and personal fulfillment can be appealing. Advertisements entice us to materialism, sexy come-ons tempt us to lust and to gratify our desires, and idealized descriptions of "the good life" prompt us to greed and self-indulgence. And all the while we are assured by financial advisors that the right investments can make our future secure.

But all these things are an illusion—a lie.

Although we live in this world, it is not our ultimate goal or our ultimate destination. Money, sex, power, and pleasure will not bring true happiness and meaning to life. Thus we must fill our minds with what is above and beyond this life—God's priorities and our eternal life with him. Or to use Jesus' words, we must "make the Kingdom of God [our] primary concern." That attitude lets God handle everything else.

Sip to take away

Don't be taken in by the lies of this world and become attached to what is temporary. Look at your few short years on earth from God's point of view, and seek what he desires. You are secure in his love.

a cup of . . .

Authority

LIVING WATER

Your word is a lamp for my feet and a light for my path.   PSALM 119:105

Such things were written in the Scriptures long ago to teach us. They give us hope and encouragement as we wait patiently for God's promises.

ROMANS 15:4

All Scripture is inspired by God and is useful to teach us what is true and to make us realize what is wrong in our lives. It straightens us out and teaches us to do what is right. It is God's way of preparing us in every way, fully equipped for every good thing God wants us to do.   2 TIMOTHY 3:16-17

Thirst-quenching
thought for the day

The owner's manual for a new car is packed with helpful information and advice, everything from how to turn on the windshield wipers to how to change a tire. The manufacturer wants to be sure that the owner has everything he or she needs to operate and maintain this expensive and complex piece of machinery.

Infinitely more valuable and complex than automobiles are human beings, special creations of their loving Creator. In a confusing and dangerous world, they need care and guidance. God has provided just that in his owner's manual, the Bible. The Bible writers were chosen by God and inspired by the Holy Spirit, so the Bible contains everything we need to know to live right. As God's Word, it teaches, prepares, and straightens us out to fully equip us "for every good thing God wants us to do."

Sip to take away

The Bible is God's instruction manual, handbook, spiritual first-aid kit, and love letter. Read it. Study it. Learn it. Apply it. And thank God that he loves you enough to give you such a profound and personal book.

a cup of . . .
Belonging

LIVING WATER

I am the good shepherd; I know my own sheep, and they know me, just as my Father knows me and I know the Father.   JOHN 10:14-15

You are not like that, for you are a chosen people. You are a kingdom of priests, God's holy nation, his very own possession. This is so you can show others the goodness of God, for he called you out of the darkness into his wonderful light. "Once you were not a people; now you are the people of God. Once you received none of God's mercy; now you have received his mercy."   1 PETER 2:9-10

Thirst-quenching
thought for the day

These passages offer the best antidote for an identity crisis or low self-esteem. Peter affirms that all those who belong to Christ are "chosen," "holy," and "his very own." Christ himself claims ownership over you.

All of this is true not because we are good in ourselves—in reality, we are lost and in darkness—but because of God's grace and mercy. We are declared forgiven, new, and good, and now we can walk in the light.

How do you feel about yourself? What defines your worth as an individual? Instead of comparing yourself to others or trying to match the world's standards for beauty or significance, find your true identity in Christ. Rejoice in the person he has made you, and declare the praises of your loving and merciful Lord.

Sip to take away
Stop for a moment and allow your soul to hear Jesus say, "You belong to me."

a cup of . . .

Blessing

LIVING WATER

May the Lord bless you and protect you. May the Lord smile on you and be gracious to you. May the Lord show you his favor and give you his peace.

NUMBERS 6:24-26

Now, all glory to God, who is able to keep you from stumbling, and who will bring you into his glorious presence innocent of sin and with great joy. All glory to him, who alone is God our Savior, through Jesus Christ our Lord. Yes, glory, majesty, power, and authority belong to him, in the beginning, now, and forevermore. Amen.

JUDE 1:24-25

Thirst-quenching
thought for the day

What a powerful blessing! What a marvelous promise—God will keep us from stumbling! We don't have to worry or try to cling tightly to God because he is holding us. And his purpose is to bring us to himself, faultless and blameless. All this is possible through our Lord Jesus Christ. He died on the cross, in our place, taking the penalty for our sin. Then he rose from the grave, defeating sin and death, and now he lives to intercede with the Father on our behalf. When we trust Christ as Savior, we are forgiven of our sins—past, present, and future—and we enter a secure relationship with God. Hallelujah!

The ancient blessing from Numbers forms a powerful prayer you can memorize and use when you pray for those you love.

Sip to take away

The doxology and benediction by Jude is a profound hymn of praise to our glorious God who has all glory, majesty, power, and authority. Make this your daily song.

a cup of ...

Boldness

LIVING WATER

"There is salvation in no one else! There is no other name in all of heaven for people to call on to save them."... Peter and John replied, "Do you think God wants us to obey you rather than him? We cannot stop telling about the wonderful things we have seen and heard."   ACTS 4:12, 19-20

I am not ashamed of this Good News about Christ. It is the power of God at work, saving everyone who believes—Jews first and also Gentiles.   ROMANS 1:16

God has not given us a spirit of fear and timidity, but of power, love, and self-discipline. So you must never be ashamed to tell others about our Lord.

2 TIMOTHY 1:7-8

Thirst-quenching
thought for the day

Emboldened by the Resurrection and empowered by the Holy Spirit, Peter and John courageously proclaimed that the only way to find forgiveness and salvation was through Jesus Christ of Nazareth. And when they were ordered by the rulers and elders to stop, they replied that they were compelled to speak because they had to obey God. Paul later exhibited that same boldness and encouraged his disciple Timothy to do likewise.

Many people don't like to hear that there is no other way to be forgiven and no other route to heaven. But it's true. Christians should be open-minded on many issues but not on how to be saved from sin. That truth is central to what we believe. No other religious teacher could take the penalty for our sins; no one else came to earth as God's only Son; no other person rose from the dead. There is no other name or way to heaven. Let us boldly proclaim this truth to the world.

Sip to take away

Whenever you feel threatened or embarrassed about sharing your faith in Christ, remember the words and example of Peter and John. Then tell the truth.

a cup of ...

Certainty

LIVING WATER

Jesus told him, "I am the way, the truth, and the life. No one can come to the Father except through me."

JOHN 14:6

There is salvation in no one else! There is no other name in all of heaven for people to call on to save them.

ACTS 4:12

This is what God has testified: He has given us eternal life, and this life is in his Son. So whoever has God's Son has life; whoever does not have his Son does not have life.

1 JOHN 5:11-12

Thirst-quenching
thought for the day

When the disciples asked Jesus how they could follow him to his "Father's home," Jesus answered that he was the *only* way. The first message in the early church echoed that same theme. Decades later, John was still summarizing the gospel with the phrase "whoever has God's Son has life."

This fact that Jesus is the only way to heaven isn't popular in our age of "it-doesn't-matter-what-you-believe-as-long-as-you're-sincere" and "all-faiths-lead-to-the-same-destination" ways of thinking. People argue that having just one way is too narrow and too limiting. In reality, it is wide enough for all who believe. Instead of arguing and worrying about its limitations, they should be grateful that there actually is a way home. When standing at a precipice and wishing to get to the other side of a great divide, we don't pout and demand that a bridge be built where we are. Instead, we travel to the bridge, grateful that there is a way across at all.

Sip to take away

Jesus is the Way—follow him. Jesus is the Truth—believe him. Jesus is the Life—live in him. There is no other bridge to the Father and to home. Put the full weight of your life on that bridge.

a cup of . . .
Challenge

LIVING WATER

I don't mean to say that I have already achieved these things or that I have already reached perfection! But I keep working toward that day when I will finally be all that Christ Jesus saved me for and wants me to be. No, dear brothers and sisters, I am still not all I should be, but I am focusing all my energies on this one thing: Forgetting the past and looking forward to what lies ahead, I strain to reach the end of the race and receive the prize for which God, through Christ Jesus, is calling us up to heaven.   PHILIPPIANS 3:12-14

Since we are surrounded by such a huge crowd of witnesses to the life of faith, let us strip off every weight that slows us down, especially the sin that so easily hinders our progress. And let us run with endurance the race that God has set before us. We do this by keeping our eyes on Jesus, on whom our faith depends from start to finish.   HEBREWS 12:1-2

Thirst-quenching
thought for the day

Paul pictures a race where the runners expend every bit of energy to win the prize. With eyes on the goal, nothing matters to them but finishing the race and finishing well. Hebrews uses that same picture to convey the long-distance nature of the Christian life.

Paul's goal was to know Christ, to be like Christ, and to be all that Christ had in mind for him. Paul had reason to forget what was behind—he had held the coats of those who had stoned Stephen (Acts 7:57-58) and had pursued Christians to imprison and kill them.

We all have shameful acts in our past, and we live with the tension between what we have been and what we want to be. Because our hope is in Christ, we can let go of the past and look ahead to what God will help us become.

Sip to take away

Don't let anything take your eyes off your goal of knowing Christ. With the focus of a dedicated athlete, lay aside everything harmful and anything that might distract you from winning God's prize.

a cup of...

Companionship

LIVING WATER

There are "friends" who destroy each other, but a real friend sticks closer than a brother. PROVERBS 18:24

Two people can accomplish more than twice as much as one; they get a better return for their labor. If one person falls, the other can reach out and help. But people who are alone when they fall are in real trouble. ECCLESIASTES 4:9-10

Run from anything that stimulates youthful lust. Follow anything that makes you want to do right. Pursue faith and love and peace, and enjoy the companionship of those who call on the Lord with pure hearts. 2 TIMOTHY 2:22

Thirst-quenching thought for the day

Mere companions are cheap and are easily found. As long as you have something they can use or enjoy (prestige, power, money, fun, food, or drink), they will hang around and follow you almost anywhere. But at the first sign of trouble, when the party ends, or when the money runs out, these fair-weather friends quickly disappear.

Unfortunately, many confuse superficial companions with real friends. There is a difference. A genuine friend stays close, even (especially) during tough times. A real friend accepts and supports, even (especially) when everyone else has left. True friendship includes sacrifice. Deep friendship lasts through the years, even (especially) when miles come between.

Sip to take away

Do you need a friend? There *is* a friend who sticks closer than a brother—his name is Jesus, and he gave his life for you. His companionship is eternal.

a cup of . . .

Compassion

LIVING WATER

*Remember this good deed also, O my God! Have
compassion on me according to your great and
unfailing love.*   NEHEMIAH 13:22

*He revealed his character to Moses and his deeds to
the people of Israel. The Lord is merciful and
gracious; he is slow to get angry and full of unfailing love.*   PSALM 103:7-8

*This change of plans upset Jonah, and he became
very angry. So he complained to the Lord about it:
"Didn't I say before I left home that you would do
this, Lord? That is why I ran away to Tarshish! I
knew that you were a gracious and compassionate
God, slow to get angry and filled with unfailing love.
I knew how easily you could cancel your plans for
destroying these people."*   JONAH 4:1-2

Thirst-quenching
thought for the day

We can learn much about a person by looking at his or her track record—how he or she has related to others in the past. Moses, Nehemiah, and Jonah knew this, which is why they could count on God to be compassionate.

When we look at how God has acted in the past and how he has related to his people, the children of Israel, we find that God is profoundly compassionate. In fact, time after time when Israel disobeyed his commands and even began to worship idols, God was slow to punish them and took them back as soon as they turned from their sin.

The fact that God is "slow to get angry" should not encourage us to take him for granted. Instead, we should remember his unending love and determine to live for him.

Sip to take away
Thank God for what he has done in the past, for Israel, for others, and for you. And live in the light of his gracious and compassionate love.

a cup of . . .

Completeness

LIVING WATER

*He will keep you strong right up to the end, and he
will keep you free from all blame on the great day
when our Lord Jesus Christ returns.*

1 CORINTHIANS 1:8

*I am sure that God, who began the good work within
you, will continue his work until it is finally
finished on that day when Christ Jesus comes back
again.*

PHILIPPIANS 1:6

*As a result, Christ will make your hearts strong,
blameless, and holy when you stand before God our
Father on that day when our Lord Jesus comes with
all those who belong to him.*

1 THESSALONIANS 3:13

Thirst-quenching
thought for the day

What God begins, he finishes. God has begun his work, his good work in you. You can be confident that he will finish what he has started.

This means that you are not complete—you are "in progress." No matter what your temperament, personality, giftedness, success, or failure, God is working "within you," making you more like his Son, Jesus (see Romans 8:29). God's work in you began when you trusted Christ as your Savior, and it will continue until you see Christ face-to-face.

When you feel incomplete, unfinished, or distressed by your shortcomings, remember God's promise and provision. Don't let your present condition rob you of the joy of knowing Christ or keep you from growing closer to him. Be patient—God is not finished with you yet.

Sip to take away
Your completeness is found in Christ. Because of him, you will be whole! Be glad in that hope.

a cup of . . .

Confidence

LIVING WATER

The Lord is for me, so I will not be afraid. What can mere mortals do to me?   PSALM 118:6

It is better to trust the Lord than to put confidence in people.   PSALM 118:8

What can we say about such wonderful things as these? If God is for us, who can ever be against us? Since God did not spare even his own Son but gave him up for us all, won't God, who gave us Christ, also give us everything else?

ROMANS 8:31-32

Thirst-quenching thought for the day

Think through the amazing recurrent theme in today's verses: God is for us!

God . . . He is the all-powerful, all-knowing, limitless, Eternal One, Creator of the universe.

God is . . . He exists, has always been, and forever will be. He lives.

God is for . . . He is good, all-loving, personal, involved in his creation, and always seeking what is best.

God is for us . . . He is on our side, cheering for us, working for us, and transforming us into the image of his Son (Romans 8:29).

No person, no power, and no problem can stand against us—not because of us, but because of who stands with us! You want proof? God sent his Son to die for us.

Sip to take away

God is for you! Live confidently and courageously in the light of that truth.

a cup of . . .

Contentment

LIVING WATER

Since I know it is all for Christ's good, I am quite content with my weaknesses and with insults, hardships, persecutions, and calamities. For when I am weak, then I am strong.   2 CORINTHIANS 12:10

I know how to live on almost nothing or with everything. I have learned the secret of living in every situation, whether it is with a full stomach or empty, with plenty or little. For I can do everything with the help of Christ who gives me the strength I need.   PHILIPPIANS 4:12-13

If we have enough food and clothing, let us be content.   1 TIMOTHY 6:8

Thirst-quenching thought for the day

Facing an impossible task? a formidable foe? an insurmountable obstacle? Paul faced many during his life: communicating the gospel to Jews, Greeks, Romans, army officers, slaves, and rulers; dealing with jealous religious leaders, hateful pagans, and corrupt politicians; surviving beatings, stonings, lashings, imprisonments, and shipwrecks; planting churches in the most unlikely locales; and training young men to be leaders in the church. Yet Paul could do all this and more because of what Christ was doing in *him.*

Paul shared his secret: he had learned to be content in Christ. Through the highs and lows, the much and the little, Paul's relationship with Christ enabled him to carry on in any circumstance in which he found himself.

Sip to take away

What has God called you to do? How far along are you in the school of contentment? The effectiveness of your service for Christ is directly related to your level of contentment in Christ.

a cup of...
Courage

LIVING WATER

I command you—be strong and courageous! Do not be afraid or discouraged. For the Lord your God is with you wherever you go.

JOSHUA 1:9

The Lord is for me, so I will not be afraid. What can mere mortals do to me?

PSALM 118:6

God has not given us a spirit of fear and timidity, but of power, love, and self-discipline.

2 TIMOTHY 1:7

Thirst-quenching
thought for the day

Self-doubt need not prevent a person from being an effective leader. What one does with self-doubt is what separates those who succeed from those who fail.

After Moses died, Joshua was given the awesome task of leading God's people, Israel, into the Promised Land. It would have been quite natural for Joshua to doubt his fitness to take over for Moses and direct a whole nation. So God reminded Joshua who was really in control, and he promised to be with him in every decision, meeting, and battle. As a result, Joshua could be "strong and courageous." David and Timothy faced similar challenges and received similar reminders to take courage. Healthy self-doubt is the kind of uncertainty that helps a leader rely on God.

Sip to take away
What battles loom on your horizon? What crucial decisions do you have to make? What relationships need your attention? Who needs your decisive leadership?

Take courage and strength from the fact that God is in control and is leading you. And he "is with you wherever you go."

a cup of . . .

Deliverance

LIVING WATER

Moses told the people, "Don't be afraid. Just stand where you are and watch the Lord rescue you. The Egyptians that you see today will never be seen again. The Lord himself will fight for you. You won't have to lift a finger in your defense!"   EXODUS 14:13-14

My eyes strain to see your deliverance, to see the truth of your promise fulfilled.   PSALM 119:123

He is my loving ally and my fortress, my tower of safety, my deliverer. He stands before me as a shield, and I take refuge in him. He subdues the nations under me.   PSALM 144:2

Thirst-quenching
thought for the day

Chances are, you don't use the word *deliverance* very often. That, however, is no indication of how often you need deliverance! God's role as our deliverer reminds us, as it did the Israelites long ago, how much we need God's help.

After suffering as slaves in Egypt for many years, the Israelites were finally allowed to leave and journey to their Promised Land. But soon after giving permission for their departure, Pharaoh changed his mind and sent his army to bring them back. Seeing the approaching army in the distance, many of the Israelites were filled with fear and began to panic. So Moses answered them with his strong prediction of how God would rescue them from their enemies.

We may not be pursued by armies, but we will have occasions when we feel chased, trapped, or under attack simply for being one of God's people. That's when we need to remember Moses' advice to stand firm and watch for God to act on our behalf. We need to watch attentively for God's help.

Sip to take away

Are you being ridiculed for your faith? Are you being pressured to act immorally or unethically? Do you feel trapped, with no way out? "Just stand where you are and watch the Lord rescue you."

a cup of . . .

Encouragement

LIVING WATER

Dear brothers and sisters, I close my letter with these last words: Rejoice. Change your ways. Encourage each other. Live in harmony and peace. Then the God of love and peace will be with you.

2 CORINTHIANS 13:11

The Lord himself will come down from heaven with a commanding shout, with the call of the archangel, and with the trumpet call of God. First, all the Christians who have died will rise from their graves. Then, together with them, we who are still alive and remain on the earth will be caught up in the clouds to meet the Lord in the air and remain with him forever. So comfort and encourage each other with these words.

1 THESSALONIANS 4:16-18

Thirst-quenching thought for the day

Paul says to "encourage each other" with this message: Jesus will return and take us to be with him forever. What a great promise! And what an encouragement.

- When you are hassled and hurt for being a Christian, remember your Lord.
- When you experience setbacks and wonder about the future, remember his promise.
- When you struggle to live for Christ in a world that is falling apart, remember that this world is not your home.
- When you grieve for dead loved ones, remember that one day all believers will be reunited.
- When you feel trapped with no way of escape, look up.
- When you are encouraged, look for others to encourage.

Sip to take away

Be encouraged because you know how the story turns out!

a cup of . . .

Endurance

LIVING WATER

Because you trusted me, I will preserve your life and keep you safe. I, the Lord, have spoken!

JEREMIAH 39:18

Even though the fig trees have no blossoms, and there are no grapes on the vine; even though the olive crop fails, and the fields lie empty and barren; even though the flocks die in the fields, and the cattle barns are empty, yet I will rejoice in the Lord! I will be joyful in the God of my salvation.

HABAKKUK 3:17-18

All these faithful ones died without receiving what God had promised them, but they saw it all from a distance and welcomed the promises of God. They agreed that they were no more than foreigners and nomads here on earth. HEBREWS 11:13

Thirst-quenching thought for the day

As Habakkuk looked at his world, he saw evil and injustice permeating every level of society. Even worse, the wicked were flourishing, reveling in their greed, flouting the laws, and oppressing the righteous. With dismay and anguish, Habakkuk cried to God, "Must I forever see this sin and misery all around me?" (Habakkuk 1:3). God answered by reminding Habakkuk that he, the Lord, was holy and just and the judge of all the earth, and that at the right time he would punish the wicked. Until then, the righteous would live by faith (Habakkuk 2:4). Hearing God's answer, Habakkuk responded with a strong statement of courage and joy; regardless of the circumstances, he would "rejoice in the Lord" and continue to live for him.

Habakkuk was one of those referred to by the writer of Hebrews who had to wait beyond death to receive what God had promised. These believers trusted God to keep his word.

Sip to take away

When you see no relief in sight and wonder *Why? How?* and *How long?* remember that the final chapter has not been written—God's justice will prevail. Rejoice in who God is, and live by faith in your strong, loving, and holy Savior.

a cup of . . .

Escape

LIVING WATER

God will surely do this for you, for he always does just what he says, and he is the one who invited you into this wonderful friendship with his Son, Jesus Christ our Lord.

1 CORINTHIANS 1:9

Remember that the temptations that come into your life are no different from what others experience. And God is faithful. He will keep the temptation from becoming so strong that you can't stand up against it. When you are tempted, he will show you a way out so that you will not give in to it.

1 CORINTHIANS 10:13

So you see, the Lord knows how to rescue godly people from their trials, even while punishing the wicked right up until the day of judgment.

2 PETER 2:9

Thirst-quenching
thought for the day

Temptation comes in various forms. There are obvious enticements to break the law, cheat, or forsake a commitment; subtle pressures to flirt with the wrong person, bend the rules, or delay doing right; and nearly invisible urgings to gratify self, compromise values, or take the easy way out. Through the constant pull of our sinful nature and the consistent attacks of our enemy, Satan, we find ourselves tempted all day and every day. Facing such powerful and continual influences, we may consider giving up and giving in.

But God is more powerful . . . and he is "faithful," promising to keep temptation from overwhelming us and to provide an alternate course of action, a way of escape, a "way out." The stronger the temptation, the more we can count on God's faithfulness!

Sip to take away

When you are tempted, thank God for trusting you that much. He knows what you can bear with his help. Then ask him what you should do next—look for his way out and take it.

a cup of . . .

Eternal Truth

LIVING WATER

Heaven and earth will disappear, but my words will remain forever.

LUKE 21:33

As the prophet says, "People are like grass that dies away; their beauty fades as quickly as the beauty of wildflowers. The grass withers, and the flowers fall away. But the word of the Lord will last forever." And that word is the Good News that was preached to you.

1 PETER 1:24-25

Thirst-quenching
thought for the day

What is completely dependable? What stands
secure in this world? Nothing. Fires destroy homes
and lives; earthquakes reduce highways to rubble;
hurricanes and tornadoes blow away dreams. Even
the strongest athlete, the most powerful politician,
the most glamorous celebrity, and the richest
tycoon eventually die.

Only "the word of the Lord," says Peter, "will last
forever." Then he adds, "And that word is the Good
News that was preached to you." If you want to
learn about eternity, look in the pages of Scripture,
God's eternal Word.

In a world of instability and insecurity, we have
the sure Word of God, the Bible. And we have the
freedom to read it, interpret it, and apply it to our
lives.

Sip to take away

Do you want to know what God is like? Do
you want to find the answers to life's most
perplexing questions? Do you want to
know how to live? Do you want a solid
foundation? Study God's Word.

a cup of . . .
Expectation

LIVING WATER

*The Kingdom of Heaven can be illustrated by the
story of a king who prepared a great wedding feast
for his son.*   MATTHEW 22:2

*Then I heard again what sounded like the shout of a
huge crowd, or the roar of mighty ocean waves, or
the crash of loud thunder: "Hallelujah! For the Lord
our God, the Almighty, reigns. Let us be glad and
rejoice and honor him. For the time has come for the
wedding feast of the Lamb, and his bride has
prepared herself. She is permitted to wear the finest
white linen." (Fine linen represents the good deeds
done by the people of God.)*   REVELATION 19:6-8

Thirst-quenching thought for the day

This passage in Revelation describes the culmination of human history—the wedding of the Lamb (Christ) and his bride (faithful believers from all time). The bride's clothing is made of the good deeds done by the people of God. It turns out that the parable Jesus told in Matthew's Gospel described a real wedding feast!

In Jesus' day, a young woman who was engaged to be married would wait expectantly for her groom to come for her. When the groom finally arrived, he and the bride, dressed exquisitely for the wedding ceremony, were joined as one. That is the biblical picture of Christ and his bride, the church. Until that glorious wedding day arrives, however, we must prepare to meet our groom, the Son of God. We prepare by staying faithful to him, living for him, telling others about him, and looking for his return.

Sip to take away
Are you ready for your wedding day?

a cup of . . .

Faith

LIVING WATER

*I assure you, anyone who believes in me already has
eternal life.*   JOHN 6:47

*Jesus told her, "I am the resurrection and the life.
Those who believe in me, even though they die like
everyone else, will live again. They are given eternal
life for believing in me and will never perish. Do you
believe this, Martha?"*   JOHN 11:25-26

*God chose him for this purpose long before the
world began, but now in these final days, he was
sent to the earth for all to see. And he did this for
you. Through Christ you have come to trust in God.
And because God raised Christ from the dead and
gave him great glory, your faith and hope can be
placed confidently in God.*   1 PETER 1:20-21

Thirst-quenching thought for the day

Faith in God is not a blind leap in the dark that defies reason. Jesus' life and death are clear evidence that God exists and that he loves us. God sent Jesus to live on the earth as a man and to die on the cross as the perfect sacrifice for our sins. His resurrection and ascension show us that he was and is God's eternal Son. We can be confident that God is true and that we will have eternal life just as he promised.

When doubts creep in, remember the facts about Jesus. When problems hit, hold on to the reality of Christ. When despair threatens to engulf you in darkness, take hope in God's promises of deliverance and eternal life. Jesus was chosen, revealed, raised, and glorified!

Sip to take away
Don't let moments of darkness cause you to forget what you saw in the light!

a cup of . . .

Faithfulness

LIVING WATER

Understand, therefore, that the Lord your God is indeed God. He is the faithful God who keeps his covenant for a thousand generations and constantly loves those who love him and obey his commands.
DEUTERONOMY 7:9

I entrust my spirit into your hand. Rescue me, Lord, for you are a faithful God.
PSALM 31:5

May the God of peace make you holy in every way, and may your whole spirit and soul and body be kept blameless until that day when our Lord Jesus Christ comes again. God, who calls you, is faithful; he will do this.
1 THESSALONIANS 5:23-24

Thirst-quenching thought for the day

How do you describe God? The Old Testament contains dozens of names for God, each one emphasizing an important aspect of his character. Each of these passages describes him as "faithful."

Faithfulness is important in any relationship. A faithful person is someone we can count on during tough times, someone who is loyal and true, and someone who keeps promises and commitments.

In contrast, *unfaithfulness* has become a primary characteristic of modern culture. Husbands and wives break marriage vows, workers and employers break commitments, skilled lawyers look for loopholes in contracts, family members abuse each other, and friendships dissolve over trivialities. We long for the security and hope that faithfulness brings.

In the biblical reminders that "he is the faithful God," we find the promise that God always keeps his commitments. And though everyone else may desert us, God will be there. Thank the Lord!

Sip to take away

In his prayer for the Thessalonians, Paul asked God to make them holy and keep them blameless. Then he assured his readers God would do that because he is faithful. God hasn't changed. He will practice that same faithfulness in your life today. What a reason for joy!

a cup of . . .

Foresight

LIVING WATER

Because of Christ, we have received an inheritance from God, for he chose us from the beginning, and all things happen just as he decided long ago.

EPHESIANS 1:11

I pray that your hearts will be flooded with light so that you can understand the wonderful future he has promised to those he called. I want you to realize what a rich and glorious inheritance he has given to his people.

EPHESIANS 1:18

We are all one body, we have the same Spirit, and we have all been called to the same glorious future.

EPHESIANS 4:4

Thirst-quenching thought for the day

At times we wish we could see into the future, especially when struggling with an important decision or wondering about the result of a certain course of action. But as finite human beings, we must live each moment, hour, and day without knowing for sure what will occur. Sometimes the future seems bright; at other times it appears bleak or threatening. Whatever the case, it is unknown.

Reading God's promise of a glorious future to those who trust in him fills us with a new zest for life. Whether we live or die, become famous or anonymous, have sickness or great health, we can be confident that God has called us to a wonderful future. And that gives us hope.

Sip to take away

You can't know the details of your future, but you can know that God ultimately has good things in store. Turn each day over to God, and live one day at a time by faith. Your future is bright!

a cup of . . .
Forever

LIVING WATER

You keep track of all my sorrows. You have collected all my tears in your bottle. You have recorded each one in your book.　　　PSALM 56:8

He will swallow up death forever! The Sovereign Lord will wipe away all tears. He will remove forever all insults and mockery against his land and people. The Lord has spoken!　　　ISAIAH 25:8

He will remove all of their sorrows, and there will be no more death or sorrow or crying or pain. For the old world and its evils are gone forever.

REVELATION 21:4

Thirst-quenching thought for the day

Everyone knows about tears. When a toddler loses a toy, a child loses a pet, a teenager loses a love, a man loses his father, or a wife loses her husband, tears threaten to overwhelm us. Yet we are not alone in our sorrow. God is with us, comforting us with his love, peace, and tender care, and promising that one day death, sorrow, dying, and pain will be abolished . . . forever!

What great sorrow do you harbor? What is your private grief? No matter what you are going through, it's not the last word—God has written the final chapter, and it includes true fulfillment and eternal joy for those who love him. Eternity with God will be more wonderful than you can ever imagine—all wrongs will be made right and all tears wiped away.

Sip to take away

Thank God for loving you so much that he keeps track of your tears!

a cup of...
Forgiveness

LIVING WATER

Oh, what joy for those whose rebellion is forgiven, whose sin is put out of sight! Yes, what joy for those whose record the Lord has cleared of sin, whose lives are lived in complete honesty! PSALM 32:1-2

You have forgiven the guilt of your people— yes, you have covered all their sins. PSALM 85:2

God was in Christ, reconciling the world to himself, no longer counting people's sins against them. This is the wonderful message he has given us to tell others. 2 CORINTHIANS 5:19

Thirst-quenching thought for the day

Imagine the exhilaration of a death-row inmate granted a stay of execution. Once condemned to die, he is shown mercy and allowed to live. Instead of awaiting execution, he is free to live out his days. He has passed from death to life!

Sin casts a similar cloud over our relationship with God. Our disobedience interrupts fellowship with God and leaves our souls in darkness. And we sinners remain guilty, awaiting our deserved punishment. Like condemned murderers, we know that the just sentence is death.

But not only is our sentence commuted, we are pardoned, forgiven, set free! That's why David exclaims enthusiastically that we are "cleared of sin." That's why God's Word so frequently returns to the subject of forgiveness. That's why Paul points out that we have a wonderful message to offer others—the good news of God's forgiveness in Christ.

Sip to take away

If you have given your life to Christ and trust in him alone for salvation, your sins are forgiven, paid for by his blood. Once condemned, now you have been pardoned! Thank God for his love and justice, and rejoice in your freedom.

a cup of...
Freedom

LIVING WATER

You will know the truth, and the truth will set you free.

JOHN 8:32

There is no condemnation for those who belong to Christ Jesus. For the power of the life-giving Spirit has freed you through Christ Jesus from the power of sin that leads to death.

ROMANS 8:1-2

Christ has really set us free. Now make sure that you stay free, and don't get tied up again in slavery to the law.

GALATIANS 5:1

Thirst-quenching thought for the day

Sin enslaves and destroys. Born sinners, we soon discover that sinning is a way of life. It's what we do naturally. We are slaves to sin from the start. But sin leads to guilt, condemnation, and death. That's the "power of sin."

In sharp contrast, Christ brings forgiveness, freedom, and life. That's the "power of the life-giving Spirit." Because you trusted Christ as your Savior, you have been released. The shackles of sin have been broken by your Lord, and you stand before God forgiven and clean. Now you have the freedom to do what is right—to obey God, and to love others in his name. And the Spirit will give you the power you need. Live for him!

Sip to take away
We stay free by staying with the one who gave us freedom.

a cup of...

Fruitfulness

LIVING WATER

My true disciples produce much fruit. This brings
great glory to my Father. JOHN 15:8

When the Holy Spirit controls our lives, he will
produce this kind of fruit in us: love, joy, peace,
patience, kindness, goodness, faithfulness, gentle-
ness, and self-control. Here there is no conflict with
the law. GALATIANS 5:22-23

Though your hearts were once full of darkness, now
you are full of light from the Lord, and your behav-
ior should show it! For this light within you
produces only what is good and right and true.

GALATIANS 5:8-9

Thirst-quenching
thought for the day

The qualities that God's Spirit brings to our lives are priceless. These qualities can't be bought or earned. We can't work them up by wishing, hoping, visualizing, or gritting our teeth with determination. And they certainly can't be legislated. They are produced in everyone who names Christ as Savior.

These qualities are by-products, or fruit, of the Holy Spirit's work in our lives. He gives us love for our enemy, joy despite our circumstances, peace in turmoil, patience amidst aggravations, kindness in a violent society, goodness when surrounded by corruption, faithfulness though commitment is scarce, gentleness amidst pushy self-centeredness, and self-control in a world of hedonism.

These qualities stand in direct opposition to what comes naturally (see Ephesians 4:17-19). They come directly from God himself.

Sip to take away

Do you want overflowing love, abounding joy, deep peace, strong patience, tender kindness, contagious goodness, enduring faithfulness, consistent gentleness, and steady self-control? Yield your will to God and allow him to work in and through you.

a cup of . . .

Fullness

LIVING WATER

I pray that Christ will be more and more at home in your hearts as you trust in him. May your roots go down deep into the soil of God's marvelous love. And may you have the power to understand, as all God's people should, how wide, how long, how high, and how deep his love really is. May you experience the love of Christ, though it is so great you will never fully understand it. Then you will be filled with the fullness of life and power that comes from God.   EPHESIANS 3:17-19

In Christ the fullness of God lives in a human body, and you are complete through your union with Christ. He is the Lord over every ruler and authority in the universe.   COLOSSIANS 2:9-10

Thirst-quenching
thought for the day

Christ's love reaches every corner of our existence. It is wide, covering the breadth of our experience and reaching the whole world. It is long, spanning the whole length of our lives. It is high, rising to the heights of honor, celebration, and elation. And it is deep, reaching to the depths of discouragement, despair, and death. No matter where we are or what we are going through, God is there, loving us and keeping us close. When we know Christ, we become rooted in the soil of God's love. And as we gain a growing awareness of God's love, we experience the fullness of life.

When you are far away from family and friends, God is there. When you feel old and alone, God is there. When you exult in a great victory, God is there. When you face defeat and despair, God is there.

Sip to take away

God loves you and wants you to be filled with his life and power.

a cup of . . .

Glory

LIVING WATER

The heavens tell of the glory of God. The skies display his marvelous craftsmanship. PSALM 19:1

The Word became human and lived here on earth among us. He was full of unfailing love and faithfulness. And we have seen his glory, the glory of the only Son of the Father. JOHN 1:14

All praise to him who loves us and has freed us from our sins by shedding his blood for us. He has made us his Kingdom and his priests who serve before God his Father. Give to him everlasting glory! He rules forever and ever! Amen! REVELATION 1:5-6

Thirst-quenching
thought for the day

By saying "give to him everlasting glory," John praises Christ by acknowledging his eternal glory and power. Overwhelmed by what Christ has done for him, John responds with enthusiastic adoration for his Lord and Savior. For John, the vision that opened Revelation was an extension of his experience with Jesus during their years together. He was an eyewitness of the glory of Jesus.

Many people hesitate to tell others of Christ because they don't feel that the change in their lives has been spectacular enough. But we should witness for Christ because of what he has done for us, not because of what we have done for him.

Think about it. Christ demonstrated his great love by freeing you from your sins through his death on the cross. He has guaranteed you a place in his kingdom and made you a priest to administer his love to others. The fact that the all-powerful God gives you eternal life is nothing short of spectacular.

 Sip to take away
Praise God through your words and actions. Start by asking God to glorify himself through you.

a cup of . . .

God's Awesomeness

LIVING WATER

The Lord Most High is awesome. He is the great King of all the earth.

PSALM 47:2

Who can comprehend the power of your anger? Your wrath is as awesome as the fear you deserve.

PSALM 90:11

O Sovereign Lord! You have made the heavens and earth by your great power. Nothing is too hard for you!

JEREMIAH 32:17

Thirst-quenching thought for the day

We may not be able to comprehend much of the nature of God, but he does reveal enough about himself that we should be in awe of him. The biblical writers also give glimpses of God's greatness. Read Jeremiah's statement again.

"O Sovereign Lord!"—what a great way to address God. It's as though the prophet is overwhelmed with God's power and lordship. We, too, can exult in the knowledge that our omnipotent God is in control of the heavens, the earth, and everything therein. Despite everything we don't know about God, we know enough to rightly proclaim him "O Sovereign Lord."

Sip to take away

For what problems do you need solutions? What important decisions do you have to make? What struggles are you facing? For which questions do you want answers? Turn to your all-powerful Creator. Nothing is too hard for him.

a cup of ...
God's Cleansing

Living Water

*"Come now, let us argue this out," says the Lord.
"No matter how deep the stain of your sins, I can
remove it. I can make you as clean as freshly fallen
snow. Even if you are stained as red as crimson, I
can make you as white as wool."*　　　ISAIAH 1:18

*Just think how much more the blood of Christ will
purify our hearts from deeds that lead to death so
that we can worship the living God.*　　　HEBREWS 9:14

*If we are living in the light of God's presence, just as
Christ is, then we have fellowship with each other,
and the blood of Jesus, his Son, cleanses us from
every sin.*　　　1 JOHN 1:7

Thirst-quenching
thought for the day

Laundry days can include a few nightmares. What's the toughest stain to remove? Grape juice? ink? coffee? mud? After soaking, scrubbing, and soaking some more, we often give up in frustration. The stain just won't come out, and the shirt is ruined!

The effects of sin run profoundly deeper than soiled clothing. Sin affects all of life, staining the soul with real guilt and painful estrangement from God. And this sin stain resists every human effort to remove it. No matter how hard we work or hope or pray, the contaminating stain remains.

The truth is that only God can cleanse us and make us truly clean. And he promises to do just that . . . through faith in his Son.

Sip to take away

Are you struggling with guilt from your sins? You can be forgiven, released, and set on the path of righteousness. For a new start and a new life, confess your sins to God and trust in Christ. His stain remover works!

a cup of . . .

God's Delight

LIVING WATER

The Lord's delight is in those who honor him, those who put their hope in his unfailing love.

PSALM 147:11

Where is another God like you, who pardons the sins of the survivors among his people? You cannot stay angry with your people forever, because you delight in showing mercy.

MICAH 7:18

The Lord your God has arrived to live among you. He is a mighty savior. He will rejoice over you with great gladness. With his love, he will calm all your fears. He will exult over you by singing a happy song.

ZEPHANIAH 3:17

Thirst-quenching thought for the day

The prophet Zephaniah predicted tough times for the nation of Judah. As punishment from God, the nation would be conquered—her cities destroyed and her people taken captive. Yet along with this bad news, Zephaniah included a message of hope. Because of God's great love for his people, he would rescue and restore them when they returned to him.

God's relationship with his people offers a framework for understanding his relationship with you. If you have trusted in Christ, you are God's—you belong to him. He loves you, takes delight in you, and rejoices over you. No matter what you have done or where you are, remember that God is with you and is your "mighty savior."

Sip to take away

Think of it. God delights in showing mercy to all who come to him in repentance! Turn back to him and let him "calm all your fears" with his love.

a cup of . . .

God's Faithfulness

LIVING WATER

Your faithfulness extends to every generation, as enduring as the earth you created.

PSALM 119:90

The unfailing love of the Lord never ends! By his mercies we have been kept from complete destruction. Great is his faithfulness; his mercies begin afresh each day.

LAMENTATIONS 3:22-23

I am the Lord, and I do not change.

MALACHI 3:6

Thirst-quenching
thought for the day

Take advantage of the patterns in your life. Morning, noon, and night—waking, working, eating, sleeping—our lives are defined by daily cycles. Each day presents fresh opportunities and challenges . . . and dangers and temptations. But as sure as the sunrise, God's "mercies begin afresh each day." He stands ready to love, forgive, and guide us through the day. Use the patterns in your life to remind you of God's faithfulness. Rely on him.

Sip to take away
Whatever you've done and whatever you face, turn to God first, each morning. Give him your day and allow him to guide each step.

a cup of . . .

God's Love

LIVING WATER

God so loved the world that he gave his only Son, so that everyone who believes in him will not perish but have eternal life.   JOHN 3:16

God showed his great love for us by sending Christ to die for us while we were still sinners.   ROMANS 5:8

God showed how much he loved us by sending his only Son into the world so that we might have eternal life through him. This is real love. It is not that we loved God, but that he loved us and sent his Son as a sacrifice to take away our sins.   1 JOHN 4:9-10

Thirst-quenching
thought for the day

Love is a popular topic. We talk about it, write about it, and sing about it. Everyone wants to love and be loved. But true love can become obscure and counterfeit unless it moves beyond talk into action. John says that we can see true love in what God did: He sent his Son, and Christ gave his life. God's love sends, gives, serves, feeds, heals, and dies. For God, love is not a passive idea, it is a passionate action! That is why Paul stresses that God "showed his great love for us by sending Christ!"

True love is centered on others. All too often when people speak of love, they are focused on *their* wants, rather than on those of another person. But again, God provides the contrasting example—Christ came to earth to give himself *for us.*

How can we respond to such sacrificial, selfless love? By loving God and others the same way (see 1 John 4:11-12).

Sip to take away

Thank God for his great love for you. Demonstrate your gratitude by giving yourself to others, just as Christ gave himself for you.

a cup of . . .

God's Omnipresence

LIVING WATER

Even when I walk through the dark valley of death, I will not be afraid, for you are close beside me.

PSALM 23:4

I can never escape from your spirit! I can never get away from your presence! If I go up to heaven, you are there; if I go down to the place of the dead, you are there. If I ride the wings of the morning, if I dwell by the farthest oceans, even there your hand will guide me, and your strength will support me.

PSALM 139:7-10

"Can anyone hide from me? Am I not everywhere in all the heavens and earth?" asks the Lord.

JEREMIAH 23:24

Thirst-quenching
thought for the day

What is omnipresence? Being everywhere, all the time. God isn't just everywhere in a general sense. Rather, God is everywhere in an immediate sense. Some people think they can run from God, moving beyond his sight or reach. They act as if they can hide their sins, disguise their true motives, and play at church. It's ridiculous, of course, because God sees and knows everything. But these men and women try to hide their guilt from God. God's Word makes his omnipresence very personal.

For those of us who know God and have experienced his love, the fact that we cannot hide from him is wonderful news. No matter where we are, he is there.

Sip to take away

Perhaps you are in uncharted waters and feel as though oceans separate you from God. Remember that your loving Father is always with you. He is ready to hold you steady in the storm, guide you, and bring you safely to his harbor.

a cup of . . .

God's Power

LIVING WATER

I, the Lord their God, will show love to the people of Judah. I will personally free them from their enemies without any help from weapons or armies.

HOSEA 1:7

Then he said to me, "This is what the Lord says to Zerubbabel: It is not by force nor by strength, but by my Spirit, says the Lord Almighty."

ZECHARIAH 4:6

A final word: Be strong with the Lord's mighty power.

EPHESIANS 6:10

Thirst-quenching thought for the day

How easy it is, when we face challenges of any kind, to turn first to our own resources. It's human nature to want to depend on our own cleverness, abilities, and strength. We want to do it ourselves. When we find ourselves in trouble or in need, we tend to suck it up, flex our muscles, and work hard. Finally, in desperation, we may turn to God, asking for his guidance and empowerment.

In contrast, God wants us to depend on him. And it only makes sense. He is all-powerful, he is all-knowing, he loves us, and, if we have trusted Christ as Savior, he has given us the Holy Spirit to live in us. Depending on God means turning to him first, listening to his Word, and then following his instructions.

Sip to take away

Are you worried? in trouble? struggling? questioning? Instead of trusting in your own strength and power, submit to the Lord Almighty.

a cup of . . .

God's Promises

LIVING WATER

Now, O Lord, do as you have promised concerning me and my family. May it be a promise that will last forever. And may your name be established and honored forever so that all the world will say, "The Lord Almighty is God over Israel!" And may the dynasty of your servant David be established in your presence. 1 CHRONICLES 17:23-24

Abraham waited patiently, and he received what God had promised. HEBREWS 6:15

By that same mighty power, he has given us all of his rich and wonderful promises. He has promised that you will escape the decadence all around you caused by evil desires and that you will share in his divine nature. 2 PETER 1:4

Thirst-quenching
thought for the day

A promise is only as good as the character of the one who makes it. When King David prayed and claimed God's promise for him and his family, he did so based on his certainty of God's character. Although David was praying for himself, his main focus was on God, that God's name would be "honored forever." David wanted his children and all his future generations to be true to the Lord and to be blessed by him.

David knew that his trust was in the same God who had kept his promise to his ancestor Abraham. Peter reminds us that we trust in that same promise-keeping God, whose timing is perfect.

Sip to take away

What do you wish for your family? What do you ask God to do for them? May your prayers focus on God's good work, that your family may honor him and enjoy his blessings forever and that God would be praised as a result.

a cup of . . .

God's Strength

LIVING WATER

I love you, Lord; you are my strength.

PSALM 18:1

The Lord helps the fallen and lifts up those bent beneath their loads. All eyes look to you for help; you give them their food as they need it. When you open your hand, you satisfy the hunger and thirst of every living thing.

PSALM 145:14-16

He gives power to those who are tired and worn out; he offers strength to the weak.

ISAIAH 40:29

Thirst-quenching thought for the day

Some loads seem too heavy to bear. Guilt, sorrow, and daily responsibilities can weigh us down and nearly crush us. At times we may feel too weak and burdened to continue. It is in these times especially that we need to remember God's promise to care for us and meet our deepest needs.

In the Psalms, David praises God for his profound goodness, emphasizing God's compassion, mercy, and love. Isaiah echoes the same thought. These attributes of the Father are experienced as God supplies strength for each day and every challenge.

Sip to take away

When you feel overwhelmed by life, turn to the Lord for strength. He will lift you up, feed you, and meet your deepest needs.

a cup of . . .
God's Thoughts

LIVING WATER

How precious are your thoughts about me, O God!
They are innumerable! I can't even count them; they
outnumber the grains of sand! And when I wake up
in the morning, you are still with me!

PSALM 139:17-18

"My thoughts are completely different from yours,"
says the Lord. "And my ways are far beyond
anything you could imagine. For just as the heavens
are higher than the earth, so are my ways higher
than your ways and my thoughts higher than your
thoughts."

ISAIAH 55:8-9

Thirst-quenching thought for the day

Scoop up a handful of sand from the beach and count the grains before they fall through your fingers. It's impossible because they are so small and so numerous. Take a guess—how many did you hold? Now multiply that number by the number of "handfuls" on that beach. The answer is beyond imagination. That is how David pictures God's thoughts—beyond our understanding or even our wildest guess. No human being could ever know the mind of God. Yet God reveals much of his thinking in his Word to us.

God's thoughts are precious to David, however, not just because of their number but because of their focus—on his great plan for the universe in general and for his creation in particular. David realizes that despite the fact that he cannot totally know or understand God, God knows and understands him.

Sip to take away

God is thinking about you . . . right now. Thank him for his unlimited knowledge and perfect plan, and turn your thoughts toward him.

a cup of . . .

God's Trustworthiness

LIVING WATER

The law of the Lord is perfect, reviving the soul. The decrees of the Lord are trustworthy, making wise the simple. PSALM 19:7

Trust in the Lord with all your heart; do not depend on your own understanding. Seek his will in all you do, and he will direct your paths. PROVERBS 3:5-6

You love him even though you have never seen him. Though you do not see him, you trust him; and even now you are happy with a glorious, inexpressible joy. Your reward for trusting him will be the salvation of your souls. 1 PETER 1:8-9

Thirst-quenching
thought for the day

Life's pathway presents us with one choice after another. It can be confusing, at times, to know what direction to take, which way to go, what decision to make. The roads seem crooked, with sudden twists, dips and rises, and hidden intersections. In an effort to choose correctly, we analyze the situation, consider our options, and then try plans A through Z. As a last resort, we request divine assistance.

But talking with God should be our *first* resort. Instead of leaning on our "own understanding"—experience and intellect—we should trust in the one who gave us our ability to think and reason. God knows us perfectly, and he knows the future. When we "seek his will," the right path will be clear and straight. The longer we trust him, the more we will find him trustworthy.

Sip to take away

Remember that God promises his direction as a result of our trust, not the other way around. Act on what is clearly before you, and trust God to work out the details down the road.

a cup of . . .

God's Ultimate Promise

LIVING WATER

Don't try to avoid responsibility by saying you didn't know about it. For God knows all hearts, and he sees you. He keeps watch over your soul, and he knows you knew! And he will judge all people according to what they have done. PROVERBS 24:12

I, the Son of Man, will come in the glory of my Father with his angels and will judge all people according to their deeds. MATTHEW 16:27

See, I am coming soon, and my reward is with me, to repay all according to their deeds.

REVELATION 22:12

Thirst-quenching
thought for the day

When Jesus ascended into heaven, the angel explained to Jesus' followers that Jesus would return. In John's vision of the future, again he heard Jesus promise to come soon. When Jesus came the first time, he came as a baby and as the "Son of Man." When he comes again, he will return as the Lord of glory, a conquering King, and a righteous Judge.

Because Christ will reward everyone according to what he or she has done, his second coming is bad news for those who have spurned him. But it is a glorious event for those who love God and have committed their lives to Christ. Wounds will be healed, wrongs made right, families reunited, bodies made whole, and justice served. No wonder John exclaimed, "Amen! Come, Lord Jesus!" (Revelation 22:20).

Sip to take away

Jesus will be returning soon. Be prepared! Get excited! Spread the news!

a cup of . . .

God's Understanding

LIVING WATER

The other criminal protested, "Don't you fear God even when you are dying? We deserve to die for our evil deeds, but this man hasn't done anything wrong."　　　LUKE 23:40-41

God made Christ, who never sinned, to be the offering for our sin, so that we could be made right with God through Christ.　　　2 CORINTHIANS 5:21

This High Priest of ours understands our weaknesses, for he faced all of the same temptations we do, yet he did not sin. So let us come boldly to the throne of our gracious God. There we will receive his mercy, and we will find grace to help us when we need it.　　　HEBREWS 4:15-16

Thirst-quenching
thought for the day

Jesus knows us, and he knows what we face. Leaving the glories of heaven, he stooped to become human—one of us. Subject to a physical body's limitations of time and space, he struggled, suffered, was tempted, and died. He knows what it means to be human from the inside out.

This understanding doesn't mean that Christ overlooks our disobedience and excuses our mistakes—we still need to turn away from sin and turn toward him. But it does mean that he feels our pain and understands what we are going through.

Now Jesus sits at the Father's right hand as our Savior, friend, and mediator. We can come boldly into the throne room, confessing our sins, admitting our needs, and asking for help.

Sip to take away

Because of Jesus' life and death, you can come to God in prayer at any time, confident that he will listen and that your loving High Priest will show you mercy and grace. Talk to the one who understands you fully.

a cup of . . .

God's Watchfulness

LIVING WATER

The Lord watches over the path of the godly, but the path of the wicked leads to destruction. PSALM 1:6

The Lord watches over those who fear him, those who rely on his unfailing love. PSALM 33:18

The Lord himself watches over you! The Lord stands beside you as your protective shade. The sun will not hurt you by day, nor the moon at night. The Lord keeps you from all evil and preserves your life. The Lord keeps watch over you as you come and go, both now and forever. PSALM 121:5-8

Thirst-quenching
thought for the day

Things that live in the wilderness survive by facing extremes. The unyielding sun scorches, sears, and withers, and living things perish quickly without shade and water. The night holds its own terrors: that is when animals attack and thieves steal.

Using the wilderness setting to illustrate his point, the writer of Psalm 121 highlights God's protection for his people. God is like an oasis in the desert and a watchful sentry at night, allowing us to work in safety and sleep in peace. God watches attentively as we "come and go"—no matter where we are. And not just now; God watches over us forever.

Sip to take away

As you go about the business of living each day, remember that God is watching over you. Turn to him in your times of need and thank him for his tender care.

a cup of...

Goodness

LIVING WATER

The Lord is good and does what is right; he shows the proper path to those who go astray.

PSALM 25:8

The Lord is good. His unfailing love continues forever, and his faithfulness continues to each generation.

PSALM 100:5

The Lord is good. When trouble comes, he is a strong refuge. And he knows everyone who trusts in him.

NAHUM 1:7

Thirst-quenching
thought for the day

You may remember a simple prayer repeated before meals as a child. "God is great. God is good. And we thank him for our food." The middle phrase echoes the first line of the three verses above—God *is* good. Those three words may be said, as a child would, easily and without thought. But they contain a profound truth. God is *good,* not evil or neutral. And his goodness is active—he "knows everyone who trusts in him," and he actively looks out for what is best for them.

Sip to take away

When you feel surrounded by violence and hatred, remember *God is good.*

When your world seems to be falling apart, remember *God is good.*

When you feel lost, abandoned, and adrift, remember *God is good.*

When loss and pain tear at your soul, remember *God is good.*

And he will be your "strong refuge."

a cup of . . .

Good News!

LIVING WATER

Sing to the Lord; bless his name. Each day proclaim the good news that he saves.

PSALM 96:2

Anyone who calls on the name of the Lord will be saved.

JOEL 2:32

God says, "At just the right time, I heard you. On the day of salvation, I helped you." Indeed, God is ready to help you right now. Today is the day of salvation.

2 CORINTHIANS 6:2

Thirst-quenching thought for the day

These tremendous promises have been fulfilled in the lives of millions of people through the centuries. Joel proclaimed salvation from God's terrible judgment. Both the psalmist and Paul declare that every day is a good day for salvation! God does not want to destroy but to heal and to save. Right up until the end of time, he will allow men and women to repent from their sins and trust in him for their salvation.

This is the Good News that we embrace and proclaim to our friends, relatives, neighbors, and coworkers. They can be saved from sin's penalty, released from sin's power, and delivered from God's judgment. What a great God we have!

Sip to take away
Are you prepared to tell someone about your own salvation?

a cup of . . .

Grace

LIVING WATER

May God our Father and the Lord Jesus Christ give you his grace and peace.

1 CORINTHIANS 1:3

By God's grace, Jesus tasted death for everyone in all the world.

HEBREWS 2:9

Grow in the special favor and knowledge of our Lord and Savior Jesus Christ. To him be all glory and honor, both now and forevermore. Amen.

2 PETER 3:18

Thirst-quenching thought for the day

The writers of the New Testament were fascinated by God's grace. Almost every letter begins and ends with a mention of God's special favor. Peter's final word of this brief letter is the same as at the beginning, encouraging believers to grow in the "special favor and knowledge" of Jesus Christ.

No matter where we are in our spiritual journey and no matter how mature we are in our relationship with Christ, our faith will be challenged. Everyone has room to grow! The more we learn about Jesus, the more we will love him. The more we experience and understand his grace (the special favor of salvation that we don't deserve and could never earn), the more we will live for him.

Sip to take away

Thank God for his grace every day! Let it motivate you to grow in knowledge and in service to him.

a cup of . . .

Guidance

LIVING WATER

He lets me rest in green meadows; he leads me beside peaceful streams. He renews my strength. He guides me along right paths, bringing honor to his name.   PSALM 23:2-3

You chart the path ahead of me and tell me where to stop and rest. Every moment you know where I am.

PSALM 139:3

"I know the plans I have for you," says the Lord. "They are plans for good and not for disaster, to give you a future and a hope."   JEREMIAH 29:11

Thirst-quenching
thought for the day

Despite advances in modern technology, no meteorologist can accurately predict the weather all the time. Despite the tireless efforts of sport statisticians, no one can know for sure the outcome of a specific contest. Despite their insight and savvy, no politician or pundit can predict international events. And no amount of intelligence or education can predict precisely how another human being will act.

The point is that no one knows the future. No one, except God. Not limited by time, God sees the beginning, the end, and the in-between. He knows all that has happened and all that will happen. But God not only knows the future, he also has great plans for those who are his. As the saying goes, we may not know what the future holds, but we know who holds the future.

Sip to take away

When you feel apprehensive or anxious about what might happen next year, next month, or the next moment, think of God's reassuring words in Jeremiah: he has good plans for your life.

a cup of . . .

Heaven

LIVING WATER

Jesus replied, "I assure you, today you will be with me in paradise."   LUKE 23:43

You do this because you are looking forward to the joys of heaven—as you have been ever since you first heard the truth of the Good News.   COLOSSIANS 1:5

All honor to the God and Father of our Lord Jesus Christ, for it is by his boundless mercy that God has given us the privilege of being born again. Now we live with a wonderful expectation because Jesus Christ rose again from the dead. For God has reserved a priceless inheritance for his children. It is kept in heaven for you, pure and undefiled, beyond the reach of change and decay.   1 PETER 1:3-4

Thirst-quenching thought for the day

Peter's words offer joy and hope in times of trouble. Peter bases his confidence on what God has done for us in Christ Jesus. The resurrection is proof that our new birth and hope are certain. Jesus is alive, and his promises are true! They remain as true as his promise to the dying thief who believed in him.

We are called to a living hope—a hope not only for the future. Eternal life begins when we trust Christ and join God's family. No matter what pain or trial we face in this life, we know that it is not our final experience. Eventually we will live with Christ forever.

God gives you new life, now and forever. You have his power and presence as you live for him each day, and you have a heavenly inheritance reserved in your name. Praise God!

Sip to take away

Get so excited about heaven that it changes the way you live today!

a cup of . . .

Help

LIVING WATER

The eyes of the Lord watch over those who do right; his ears are open to their cries for help.

PSALM 34:15

I look up to the mountains—does my help come from there? My help comes from the Lord, who made the heavens and the earth!

PSALM 121:1-2

Our help is from the Lord, who made the heavens and the earth.

PSALM 124:8

Thirst-quenching thought for the day

In the ancient world, idols were often placed in high places—at the tops of mountains and hills. During times of calamity, distress, or war, people would look to the hills for their rescue, relying on these false gods for salvation. Psalm 121 points out the futility of that gesture. Help doesn't come from the mountains; it comes from the one who made the mountains!

Today we don't build altars on hills, but as in the days of the psalmists, we do look to a variety of places for help. We may depend on the government, a large corporation, money, family, or friends. No matter how powerful or influential, all of those forces and allies are impotent when compared to our awesome God. He alone brings us forgiveness and salvation.

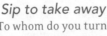

Sip to take away

To whom do you turn for help? Why not turn to the one who created all that exists? Don't look to the hills; look to your Maker.

a cup of...

Hope

LIVING WATER

Jesus replied, "People soon become thirsty again after drinking this water. But the water I give them takes away thirst altogether. It becomes a perpetual spring within them, giving them eternal life."

JOHN 4:13-14

The one sitting on the throne said, "Look, I am making all things new!" And then he said to me, "Write this down, for what I tell you is trustworthy and true." And he also said, "It is finished! I am the Alpha and the Omega—the Beginning and the End. To all who are thirsty I will give the springs of the water of life without charge!"

REVELATION 21:5-6

Thirst-quenching
thought for the day

Before the beginning of time there was God, the Creator and Sustainer of all there is. After everything has passed away, God will be there still. He is the "Beginning and the End." He is the "perpetual spring" of living water and eternal life.

Sometimes we are confronted with hatred, violence, lust, and pride at every turn. But what we presently see will not last. God will have the final word, "making all things new." As his children, we can look forward to a new heaven and earth and to eternal fellowship with our Lord.

Sip to take away
When you are thirsty, when you are discouraged, when you see no escape, look to the one who gives "the springs of the water of life without charge!"

a cup of . . .
Humility

Living Water

If my people who are called by my name will humble themselves and pray and seek my face and turn from their wicked ways, I will hear from heaven and will forgive their sins and heal their land.

2 Chronicles 7:14

Have mercy on me, O God, because of your unfailing love. Because of your great compassion, blot out the stain of my sins. Wash me clean from my guilt. Purify me from my sin. Psalm 51:1-2

If we say we have no sin, we are only fooling ourselves and refusing to accept the truth. But if we confess our sins to him, he is faithful and just to forgive us and to cleanse us from every wrong.

1 John 1:8-9

Thirst-quenching thought for the day

How tempting it is to define sin in terms of what other people do! The fact that "everyone is doing it" is no excuse for our own behavior. It's easy to list the sins of today: crime, abuse, family disintegration, racism, sexual immorality, greed, corruption, violence—the list goes on. But it's difficult to propose a cure. Political reform, harsh sentencing, government spending, and other programs have been tried but with limited success. It is difficult to accept personal responsibility for sin's presence in the world.

In these passages, God points out the only sure route to healing: humility followed by repentance and faith. God promises to cure our sin-disease if we turn away from our selfish "me first" attitudes, turn away from our sin, and turn toward him. The prescription seems simple enough, but it is profound . . . and it begins with us.

Sip to take away

Take God at his word and ask for a spirit of humility and responsibility regarding sin. When you pray for the healing of our land, ask God to begin that work in you.

a cup of . . .

Immutability

LIVING WATER

God is not a man, that he should lie. He is not a
human, that he should change his mind.

NUMBERS 23:19

"I am the Lord, and I do not change. That is why you
descendants of Jacob are not already completely
destroyed. Ever since the days of your ancestors,
you have scorned my laws and failed to obey them.
Now return to me, and I will return to you," says the
Lord Almighty.

MALACHI 3:6-7

Whatever is good and perfect comes to us from God
above, who created all heaven's lights. Unlike them,
he never changes or casts shifting shadows.

JAMES 1:17

Thirst-quenching thought for the day

If you haven't felt very close to God lately, guess who moved? It wasn't God.

That's what *immutable* means: unchanging. God is consistent, faithful, and trustworthy. In fact, that's why he didn't destroy Israel (the "descendants of Jacob") even though they had turned and moved far away from him. But God had promised to keep his promise (covenant) to his people. God's character doesn't shift like shadows or like human nature.

We move away from God when we stop talking to him, stop applying Scripture to our lives, and start living only for ourselves. When we rationalize our behavior, we fool ourselves into thinking that God has changed and that he doesn't really care how we live.

But God doesn't change. And, as our concerned and loving Father, he waits for us to return to him again.

Sip to take away

Return to the Lord and he will return to you, just as he promised his people long ago.

a cup of . . .

Inseparability

LIVING WATER

*My sheep recognize my voice; I know them, and they
follow me. I give them eternal life, and they will
never perish. No one will snatch them away from
me.*
JOHN 10:27-28

*I am convinced that nothing can ever separate us
from his love. Death can't, and life can't. The angels
can't, and the demons can't. Our fears for today, our
worries about tomorrow, and even the powers of
hell can't keep God's love away. Whether we are
high above the sky or in the deepest ocean, nothing
in all creation will ever be able to separate us from
the love of God that is revealed in Christ Jesus our
Lord.*
ROMANS 8:38-39

Thirst-quenching
thought for the day

Loneliness is an epidemic. Cut off and separated
from loving relationships—by divorce, death,
conflict, or circumstances—people feel isolated.
Even surrounded by happy, smiling faces in a
crowd, at a party, or in church, individuals can feel
lonely. Often we allow that sense of isolation to
carry over into our relationship with God.

Is that how you feel—as though no one really
knows or cares about you? Whatever the cause of
your loneliness, remember that God is with you. He
loves you; he cares for you; he's close to you. And
remember that nothing can separate you from God.
You have his word on it!

Sip to take away
During moments of loneliness, make it a
point to turn to God, remembering that
nothing can separate you from his love.

a cup of . . .

Intimacy with God

LIVING WATER

*O Lord, you have examined my heart and know
everything about me. You know when I sit down or
stand up. You know my every thought when far
away.*   PSALM 139:1-2

*How precious are your thoughts about me, O God!
They are innumerable!*   PSALM 139:17

*This is what the Lord says: "Let not the wise man
gloat in his wisdom, or the mighty man in his might,
or the rich man in his riches. Let them boast in this
alone: that they truly know me and understand that
I am the Lord who is just and righteous, whose love
is unfailing, and that I delight in these things. I, the
Lord, have spoken!"*   JEREMIAH 9:23-24

Thirst-quenching thought for the day

What if someone knew

   . . . your deepest thoughts.

   . . . your true motives.

   . . . everything about your past.

   . . . your talents, abilities, and gifts.

   . . . your dreams and desires.

Would you feel threatened? afraid? embarrassed? relieved?

God knows. He has "examined" you. He understands who you are, what you have done, and why you do what you do. He even knows your secrets, and he stands ready to forgive, guide, and protect you, and conform you to the image of his Son.

Sip to take away
Follow God's ways. Make it your life's purpose to be the person described in Jeremiah. God knows and wants what's best for you. He wants to be known by you.

a cup of . . .

Joy

LIVING WATER

*Shout to the Lord, all the earth; break out in praise
and sing for joy!*   PSALM 98:4

*Shout with joy to the Lord, O earth! Worship the
Lord with gladness. Come before him, singing with
joy. Acknowledge that the Lord is God! He made us,
and we are his. We are his people, the sheep of his
pasture.*   PSALM 100:1-3

*We were filled with laughter, and we sang for joy.
And the other nations said, "What amazing things
the Lord has done for them." Yes, the Lord has done
amazing things for us! What joy!*   PSALM 126:2-3

Thirst-quenching
thought for the day

Happiness may or may not happen; joy is the result of living as our Creator intended us to live. Happiness doesn't hold up under pressure or problems; joy doesn't let feelings get the final word on life. Joy let's God have the last word.

What did David mean by his declaration, "the Lord is God"? God is all-knowing, all-powerful, ever present, and perfect in love and in justice. Our God is eternal and not limited by time or space. He knows us completely—inside and out—past, present, and future.

With this knowledge, no wonder the writer of Psalm 100 felt moved to "shout with joy," "worship the Lord," and "come before him, singing with joy." His life was not based on what was going on within him, but on knowing that God was in control.

Sip to take away

God created you. He loves you, cares for you, and wants only the best for you. How does that make you feel? What does it prompt you to do?

a cup of...
Justice

LIVING WATER

For the Lord is righteous, and he loves justice. Those who do what is right will see his face.

PSALM 11:7

I will sing of your love and justice. I will praise you, Lord, with songs.

PSALM 101:1

I, the Lord, love justice. I hate robbery and wrongdoing. I will faithfully reward my people for their suffering and make an everlasting covenant with them.

ISAIAH 61:8

Thirst-quenching thought for the day

There's no question that this world is filled with great injustice. The poor are oppressed and the innocent condemned, while the evil and the guilty go free. Life is not fair, and often the "good guys" lose. When we experience injustice firsthand, we may be tempted to strike back and settle the score.

Those are the world's solutions to injustice—getting even, getting your way, getting what's coming to you.

But God says to be patient . . . to wait for him. God, the perfect judge, will punish the wicked and right all wrongs in his perfect timing.

 Sip to take away

Do you feel persecuted or unjustly judged? Don't take justice into your own hands. Wait for God, and he will "faithfully reward" you.

a cup of . . .

Justification

LIVING WATER

God sent Jesus to take the punishment for our sins and to satisfy God's anger against us. We are made right with God when we believe that Jesus shed his blood, sacrificing his life for us.   ROMANS 3:25

We are made right with God through faith and not by obeying the law.   ROMANS 3:28

Since we have been made right in God's sight by faith, we have peace with God because of what Jesus Christ our Lord has done for us. Because of our faith, Christ has brought us into this place of highest privilege where we now stand, and we confidently and joyfully look forward to sharing God's glory.   ROMANS 5:1-3

Thirst-quenching thought for the day

Remember, as a child, getting caught disobeying a direct instruction? You were guilty, caught red-handed, and you knew it. And you had to accept your punishment.

Through the years, circumstances change, but the pattern is the same—disobedience, guilt, punishment. Sin takes many forms—gossip, pride, lust, selfishness—and has the potential to hurt widely and deeply. Every sin is a defiance of God's laws and an affront to his holiness. The deserved punishment for our sins is death—eternal death—separation from God forever. But these passages tell us we can be "made right" with God—declared not guilty.

No matter what we have done, as Christians we have been forgiven because of Jesus. We have "peace with God" and stand in a "place of highest privilege." Not only has God declared us not guilty, he has drawn us to himself. Instead of being his enemies, we become his friends—in fact, his very own children.

Sip to take away

If you ask Jesus for forgiveness from your sins, you are freed from sin's shackles and guilt's burden. You are free to serve your loving Lord!

a cup of...
Life

LIVING WATER

*Jesus told her, "I am the resurrection and the life.
Those who believe in me, even though they die like
everyone else, will live again. They are given eternal
life for believing in me and will never perish. Do you
believe this, Martha?"* JOHN 11:25-26

*Jesus told him, "I am the way, the truth, and the life.
No one can come to the Father except through me."*
JOHN 14:6

*I myself no longer live, but Christ lives in me. So I
live my life in this earthly body by trusting in the
Son of God, who loved me and gave himself for me.*
GALATIANS 2:20

Thirst-quenching thought for the day

Standing near their brother's tomb, Mary and Martha grieved their loss. Martha questioned Jesus' timing: "If you had been here, my brother would not have died!" (John 11:21).

But Jesus is never late, and he gently reminded Martha of his awesome power and limitless love. "I am the resurrection and the life," he said. Then he called to Lazarus, the dead man, and commanded him to come forth. Lazarus did so, still wrapped in his burial clothes.

What loss threatens to unravel your life? As you stand among the gravestones, what questions or doubts do you have for the Lord? Remember, Jesus is never late. In his infinite understanding, perfect timing, and deep concern, he will hear your cry and answer your prayer. In the meantime, keep resting in his sovereignty and trusting in his love.

Sip to take away
If you have Jesus, you really have life!

a cup of...
Light

LIVING WATER

Life itself was in him, and this life gives light to everyone.

JOHN 1:4

The one who is the true light, who gives light to everyone, was going to come into the world.

JOHN 1:9

Jesus said to the people, "I am the light of the world. If you follow me, you won't be stumbling through the darkness, because you will have the light that leads to life."

JOHN 8:12

Thirst-quenching thought for the day

Everyone knows that darkness evokes fear. Like children conjuring imaginary monsters in the closet, we often allow the dark times of life to paralyze us with such fear that we begin to wonder if we can even survive.

Darkness can discourage and depress. Without light and hope, we wonder if there is any way out. Darkness fosters doubt. Unable to see, we can easily stumble and fall. Darkness comes in many forms: economic loss, personal tragedy, crippling illness, persistent sin. . . .

But Jesus is the light of the world. His presence brightens the day. His words give understanding and hope. His sacrifice brings forgiveness and eternal life. His promises of love provide certainty and security.

Sip to take away
Don't walk in darkness; follow the light.

a cup of...

Lightheartedness

LIVING WATER

Those who wait on the Lord will find new strength.
They will fly high on wings like eagles. They will run
and not grow weary. They will walk and not faint.

ISAIAH 40:31

Take my yoke upon you. Let me teach you, because I
am humble and gentle, and you will find rest for
your souls. For my yoke fits perfectly, and the
burden I give you is light. MATTHEW 11:29-30

That is why we never give up. Though our bodies are
dying, our spirits are being renewed every day. For
our present troubles are quite small and won't last
very long. Yet they produce for us an immeasurably
great glory that will last forever! 2 CORINTHIANS 4:16-17

Thirst-quenching
thought for the day

Do you ever feel overwhelmed by life? exhausted?
frustrated? discouraged? Even the strongest people
get tired at times. But God's power and strength
never diminish. God is never too tired or too busy to
listen and help you. And his strength is available
for you.

Whether we are busying ourselves in obedience
to Christ or facing life's troubles, Jesus promises
rest for our souls. When we attempt to live by our
own strength we quickly discover that life can pile
on us more than we can bear. God promises never to
do that (see 1 Corinthians 10:13)!

Sip to take away

When you feel life crushing you and
cannot go another step, remember that
you can call upon God to renew your
strength.

a cup of . . .

Majesty

Living Water

In a great chorus they sang, "Holy, holy, holy is the Lord Almighty! The whole earth is filled with his glory!"
ISAIAH 6:3

Suddenly, the angel was joined by a vast host of others—the armies of heaven—praising God: "Glory to God in the highest heaven, and peace on earth to all whom God favors. "
LUKE 2:13-14

All the angels were standing around the throne and around the elders and the four living beings. And they fell face down before the throne and worshiped God. They said, "Amen! Blessing and glory and wisdom and thanksgiving and honor and power and strength belong to our God forever and forever. Amen!"
REVELATION 7:11-12

Thirst-quenching thought for the day

Whether we consider Isaiah's vision of God's throne room, the visit of the angels to the shepherds outside Bethlehem, and John's great vision, we see the angels bowing before God's throne, worshiping and honoring him. God's majesty is overwhelming!

What has God done for you? He has sent his only Son to die for you. He has forgiven you and rescued you from sin. He has filled you with his Spirit. He has promised you eternal life after death! Respond in awe and in humble adoration, and give God honor as your King, Lord, and Savior!

Sip to take away
Ask God to give you a growing awareness of his majesty.

a cup of . . .

Meaning

LIVING WATER

We know that God causes everything to work together for the good of those who love God and are called according to his purpose for them.

ROMANS 8:28

We are pressed on every side by troubles, but we are not crushed and broken. We are perplexed, but we don't give up and quit. We are hunted down, but God never abandons us. We get knocked down, but we get up again and keep going.   2 CORINTHIANS 4:8-9

God blesses the people who patiently endure testing. Afterward they will receive the crown of life that God has promised to those who love him.   JAMES 1:12

Thirst-quenching thought for the day

Life often invites the universal question "Why?"

Why? we wonder as we struggle to put a broken relationship back together.

Why? we think as we read of a devastating earthquake halfway around the world.

Why? we sob as we stand at the grave of a loved one.

Life is short and often tragic; we are reminded of our finiteness every day. We don't know the future, we don't know the relationships between events, and we certainly don't know *why.* But we do know that God is good and all-knowing. Nothing catches him by surprise—not the car careening out of control, the malignant tumor, the hurricane, the marital breakup. So even as we question the reasons behind those events we don't understand, we can be confident that God is at work in it all.

Sip to take away

Ask God to remind you that he "causes everything to work together for the good of those who love God." He is in control!

a cup of . . .
New Life

LIVING WATER

All who believe in God's Son have eternal life.

JOHN 3:36

What this means is that those who become Christians become new persons. They are not the same anymore, for the old life is gone. A new life has begun!

2 CORINTHIANS 5:17

Whoever has God's Son has life; whoever does not have his Son does not have life.

1 JOHN 5:12

Thirst-quenching thought for the day

"New and improved!"
"The latest and best!"
"State of the art!"
Advertisers use these and similar phrases because they sell. What have advertisers discovered about people? People want what is fresh, current, and "now."

In their hearts, most people also desire a new life, a fresh start, a new beginning. That's exactly what Christ offers. In him, old things are gone and forgotten, and all things are new. Christ gives . . .

- new outlook and perspective.

- new desires and motives.

- new direction and purpose.

- new destination.

Sip to take away
It's true! Spread the NEWs that Christ offers life in all its fullness.

a cup of . . .

Outlook

LIVING WATER

Be humble and gentle. Be patient with each other, making allowance for each other's faults because of your love.   EPHESIANS 4:2

Be kind to each other, tenderhearted, forgiving one another, just as God through Christ has forgiven you.   EPHESIANS 4:32

Since God chose you to be the holy people whom he loves, you must clothe yourselves with tenderhearted mercy, kindness, humility, gentleness, and patience. You must make allowance for each other's faults and forgive the person who offends you. Remember, the Lord forgave you, so you must forgive others.   COLOSSIANS 3:12-13

Thirst-quenching
thought for the day

One great thing about adoption is that the child is greatly wanted by his or her adoptive parents. Typically the parents have waited a long time for a child, and they are thrilled to receive a new life into their home.

The Bible uses a similar picture to illustrate our relationship with the Father. We are his adopted sons and daughters—chosen by God himself—and given new life. In these passages, Paul affirms the relationship and describes this new life as God's children. He says that we are to be tenderhearted, kind, humble, gentle, patient, forgiving, loving, peaceable, and thankful (see Colossians 3:14-15). Since we have been graciously adopted, we ought to respond by showing grace to others, just as we have been shown grace by God.

Sip to take away

When you feel insignificant or lonely, remember that you are the child of a heavenly Father who chose you and loves you very much. Then demonstrate that love to others!

a cup of . . .

Peace

LIVING WATER

*You will keep in perfect peace all who trust in you,
whose thoughts are fixed on you!*   ISAIAH 26:3

*I am leaving you with a gift—peace of mind and
heart. And the peace I give isn't like the peace the
world gives. So don't be troubled or afraid.*

JOHN 14:27

*If you do this, you will experience God's peace,
which is far more wonderful than the human mind
can understand. His peace will guard your hearts
and minds as you live in Christ Jesus.*

PHILIPPIANS 4:7

Thirst-quenching thought for the day

Our lives are filled with fears, pressures, bills, busyness, emergencies, and noise. They rob us of peace of mind and soul as we rush to the next appointment and fight for sanity in a world that seems to be going insane. How in the world do we cope with it all?

Isaiah gives us the answer: The way to peace is a mind "fixed" on God. Fixed means strong and focused, not allowing anything or anyone to distract us or to move us off course.

When your world is falling apart, trust God to keep you together. When your future seems bleak, trust God to give you joy and hope. When you are surrounded by trouble and see no way out, trust God to lead you through. Trusting in our great God will bring you perfect peace.

Sip to take away

Ask the Lord to remind you that he is the ultimate source of peace.

a cup of . . .

Perseverance

LIVING WATER

There are different ways God works in our lives, but it is the same God who does the work through all of us. 1 CORINTHIANS 12:6

Dearest friends, you were always so careful to follow my instructions when I was with you. And now that I am away you must be even more careful to put into action God's saving work in your lives, obeying God with deep reverence and fear. For God is working in you, giving you the desire to obey him and the power to do what pleases him.

PHILIPPIANS 2:12-13

You, Timothy, belong to God; so run from all these evil things, and follow what is right and good. Pursue a godly life, along with faith, love, perseverance, and gentleness. 1 TIMOTHY 6:11

Thirst-quenching thought for the day

It was easy for the Philippian Christians to live for Christ when the apostle Paul was with them. The great missionary and teacher shared the Good News, modeled courageous faith, answered questions, and explained the Word. He also held the believers accountable for their beliefs and actions. But with Paul gone, it became easy to doubt, quarrel, get discouraged, and fall back into sinful habits. So Paul wrote of the seriousness of the Philippians' commitment to Christ—they should live obedient lives "with deep reverence and fear." But Paul also told them that they would not be alone. God was working in them—changing their desires and giving them the power to obey him.

Paul emphasized this in letters he wrote to other Christians. He wanted them to remember that the Christian life is a joint project: God works in and through us.

Sip to take away
Realize that your spiritual growth does not depend on you but on God's work in you. Stay in touch with him!

a cup of . . .

Persistence

LIVING WATER

Yes, I am the vine; you are the branches. Those who remain in me, and I in them, will produce much fruit. For apart from me you can do nothing.

JOHN 15:5

We have been greatly comforted, dear brothers and sisters, in all of our own crushing troubles and suffering, because you have remained strong in your faith. It gives us new life, knowing you remain strong in the Lord.

1 THESSALONIANS 3:7-8

You must remain faithful to what you have been taught from the beginning. If you do, you will continue to live in fellowship with the Son and with the Father.

1 JOHN 2:24

Thirst-quenching thought for the day

The purpose of an apple tree is to bear apples. The purpose of a cherry tree is to bear cherries. The purpose of a grapevine is to bear grapes. Christians are also expected to bear fruit: love, joy, peace, patience, kindness, goodness, faithfulness, gentleness, and self-control (see Galatians 5:22-23).

Jesus says he is the vine and believers are the branches. The secret to our bearing fruit is staying attached to the vine. Jesus' point is that we must depend on him if we hope to grow in him and be fruitful. Just as we could not become God's children on our own, we cannot bear fruit by working for it on our own. Instead, we must allow Christ to produce his fruit through us. The secret is in "remaining."

Sip to take away

We remain in Christ by communicating with him, doing what he says, and living by faith. So stay close, be nourished, and bear fruit.

a cup of...
Power

LIVING WATER

Jesus came and told his disciples, "I have been given complete authority in heaven and on earth. Therefore, go and make disciples of all the nations, baptizing them in the name of the Father and the Son and the Holy Spirit."   MATTHEW 28:18-19

With my authority, take this message of repentance to all the nations, beginning in Jerusalem: "There is forgiveness of sins for all who turn to me."

LUKE 24:47

When the Holy Spirit has come upon you, you will receive power and will tell people about me everywhere—in Jerusalem, throughout Judea, in Samaria, and to the ends of the earth.   ACTS 1:8

Thirst-quenching thought for the day

In his last statements to his disciples, Jesus promised that the Holy Spirit would come to them, that they would receive power and be his witnesses throughout the world. A few verses later, we see the fulfillment of that promise (see Acts 2:1-47). Filled with the Holy Spirit, the disciples courageously preached the gospel, and thousands responded. Then the church began to spread from Jerusalem into Judea and Samaria and then around the world.

Notice the progression of Christ's promise: power to witness comes *after* receiving the Holy Spirit. Too often we try to reverse the order, witnessing by our own power and authority. Witnessing is not showing what we can do for God; it is showing and telling what God has done for us. It is the outpouring of the Holy Spirit at work in our lives.

Sip to take away

Submit yourself completely to the Holy Spirit and watch God work through you to witness powerfully to your family, friends, neighbors, and coworkers. God wants to use you to change the world.

a cup of . . .

Praise

LIVING WATER

The Levites appointed Heman son of Joel, Asaph son of Berekiah, and Ethan son of Kushaiah from the clan of Merari to direct the musicians.

1 CHRONICLES 15:17

Your unfailing love, O Lord, is as vast as the heavens; your faithfulness reaches beyond the clouds.

PSALM 36:5

I will sing of the tender mercies of the Lord forever! Young and old will hear of your faithfulness. Your unfailing love will last forever. Your faithfulness is as enduring as the heavens.

PSALM 89:1-2

Thirst-quenching thought for the day

Ethan was one of the head musicians in the temple. He wrote Psalm 89 to celebrate God's promise to keep David's descendants on the throne forever. He may have been inspired by David's own expression of the same idea in Psalm 36, a psalm that includes an ancient note "for the choir director."

Years after these psalms were written, Jerusalem was destroyed. The history of that region is one of continual chaos, and today kings no longer rule over Israel. But the ancient psalm writers had it right: God's promise of unfailing love was fulfilled through David's greatest descendant, Jesus. God always keeps his promises. Even when the future looks bleak and the situation is confusing, we can count on him.

Sip to take away

Reflect on how God led you to himself and has cared for you over the years. Remember his faithfulness and give him praise. You may even want to break into song!

a cup of...

Priorities

LIVING WATER

To me, living is for Christ, and dying is even better.

PHILIPPIANS 1:21

I once thought all these things were so very important, but now I consider them worthless because of what Christ has done. Yes, everything else is worthless when compared with the priceless gain of knowing Christ Jesus my Lord. I have discarded everything else, counting it all as garbage, so that I may have Christ and become one with him. I no longer count on my own goodness or my ability to obey God's law, but I trust Christ to save me. For God's way of making us right with himself depends on faith.

PHILIPPIANS 3:7-9

Thirst-quenching thought for the day

When Paul spoke of what was once important to him, he was referring to his credentials, his deeds, and his heritage. But Paul considered all these things as "garbage" when compared with the greatness of knowing Christ. His relationship with Christ was more important than anything else in life. This was more than talk for Paul—he lived it. Paul was stoned, beaten, pursued, and jailed; he lost prestige, money, power, and freedom for the gospel. Still, he continued to live for Christ and share the Good News wherever he went.

To know Christ should be our ultimate goal as well. Nothing else should come close in value. No other priority will put life in its proper perspective.

Sip to take away

What is important to you? What stands in the way of knowing Christ Jesus your Lord? It's not worth it—especially when you consider what he gave for you.

a cup of . . .

Protection

LIVING WATER

You are my strength; I wait for you to rescue me, for you, O God, are my place of safety.

PSALM 59:9

My life is an example to many, because you have been my strength and protection.

PSALM 71:7

The Lord is my fortress; my God is a mighty rock where I can hide.

PSALM 94:22

Thirst-quenching thought for the day

Sometimes don't you just want a place to escape and hide from the problems, pressures, and cares of this world? A place you would feel secure and shielded from harm? To that place you could retreat and find rest and restoration. The psalmist who wrote Psalm 94 described God this way using the image of a "mighty rock where I can hide."

The psalmist tells of arrogant and evil people in positions of power who continually threaten and attack. The psalmist expresses anger, fear, and anxiety. Yet the psalmist concludes with stirring lines of hope and resolve. He remembers that God will be his strong "fortress," providing security and defense.

Sip to take away

When you are under attack, especially from those in authority over you, take refuge in God and his Word. He will protect you.

a cup of . . .
Purpose

LIVING WATER

Praise him, sun and moon! Praise him, all you twinkling stars!   PSALM 148:3

Those who are wise will shine as bright as the sky, and those who turn many to righteousness will shine like stars forever.   DANIEL 12:3

In everything you do, stay away from complaining and arguing, so that no one can speak a word of blame against you. You are to live clean, innocent lives as children of God in a dark world full of crooked and perverse people. Let your lives shine brightly before them.   PHILIPPIANS 2:14-15

Thirst-quenching
thought for the day

Do you want to be a star? Everyone these days seems to be searching for fame and fortune—sending home videos to TV producers, calling radio talk shows, and pushing to get on camera during live interviews. Perhaps the drive for significance is what motivates otherwise mature adults to act foolish to get their fifteen seconds of publicity. In reality, most celebrities quickly fade from our memories. Can you name the current Miss America? the winner of the Super Bowl two years ago? last year's Oscar winner for "Best Actor"? Oh, it's nice to be recognized, to win awards, and to be popular, but fame is not worth giving one's life for.

If you really want to be a star in the eyes of the only one whose opinion truly counts, check out Daniel's prophecy and Paul's words to the Philippians. God's stars are wise and "turn many to righteousness." Instead of drawing attention to themselves, they draw attention to Christ.

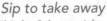 ### Sip to take away
Think of those with whom you can share the marvelous news of God's love and forgiveness in Christ. Shine on!

a cup of . . .

Refreshment

LIVING WATER

I have given rest to the weary and joy to the sorrow-ing.
JEREMIAH 31:25

I will be to Israel like a refreshing dew from heaven. It will blossom like the lily; it will send roots deep into the soil like the cedars in Lebanon.
HOSEA 14:5

Now turn from your sins and turn to God, so you can be cleansed of your sins. Then wonderful times of refreshment will come from the presence of the Lord, and he will send Jesus your Messiah to you again.
ACTS 3:19-20

Thirst-quenching
thought for the day

Jeremiah, like prophets before and after him, predicted that God's chosen people would be conquered and taken captive. The nation then would be brought back from captivity and restored completely. That pattern was repeated by Hosea and centuries later by Peter. After God confronts sin and warns of punishment, he always adds a note of grace and hope.

Soon after Jeremiah's prophecy was given, the first part was fulfilled: The army of Nebuchadnezzar besieged Jerusalem, conquered it, and took many of its citizens back to Babylon. Imagine what those captives must have been thinking and what they must have felt. Did they continue to trust in God? Did they remember God's promise of restoration?

Although you probably have not been conquered by a foreign army, you may feel defeated or in captivity. A load of bills, obligations, and responsibilities weigh heavily on you, draining your strength and exhausting your reserves. But remember that God is your source of refreshment and rest.

Sip to take away
Keep obeying God's Word. Keep trusting in his love. God will restore you!

a cup of . . .

Refuge

LIVING WATER

The Lord is a shelter for the oppressed, a refuge in times of trouble. Those who know your name trust in you, for you, O Lord, have never abandoned anyone who searches for you.   PSALM 9:9-10

The Lord looked and was displeased to find that there was no justice. He was amazed to see that no one intervened to help the oppressed. So he himself stepped in to save them with his mighty power and justice.   ISAIAH 59:15-16

God has given us both his promise and his oath. These two things are unchangeable because it is impossible for God to lie. Therefore, we who have fled to him for refuge can take new courage, for we can hold on to his promise with confidence.   HEBREWS 6:18

Thirst-quenching
thought for the day

How often do you use the word *oppressed* in conversation? Our unfamiliarity with the word reflects the invisibility of such people in our lives. The oppressed in society are often those who are poor, disadvantaged, naive, and needy. They are at the mercy of slum landlords who exact high rent for substandard housing, domineering employers who exploit their workers, ruthless dictators who line their pockets with tax revenues, conscienceless adults who mercilessly abuse children. Oppressors hope to keep the oppressed "in their place," out of the way.

Around the world believers increasingly are numbered among the oppressed. Many manage to live for Christ in their difficult situations. Others work in Christ's name to relieve suffering, bandage wounds, feed, and teach. Many have been persecuted and oppressed simply because they follow Jesus. Whatever the case, this passage rings with hope for all who are under an oppressive heel—God promises to be their refuge.

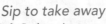

Sip to take away

Ask God to give you a sensitive heart for the oppressed. Make it a point to pray for them, and see what else you might do for them.

a cup of . . .

Relationship

LIVING WATER

Let them boast in this alone: that they truly know me and understand that I am the Lord who is just and righteous, whose love is unfailing, and that I delight in these things. I, the Lord, have spoken!

JEREMIAH 9:24

Oh, that we might know the Lord! Let us press on to know him! Then he will respond to us as surely as the arrival of dawn or the coming of rains in early spring.

HOSEA 6:3

You see, it is impossible to please God without faith. Anyone who wants to come to him must believe that there is a God and that he rewards those who sincerely seek him.

HEBREWS 11:6

Thirst-quenching
thought for the day

We live in a world of change and decay. Possessions break and rust. People disappoint and desert. Homes crumble and burn. Advertisers and politicians promise and then forget. In the midst of all that, we can feel insecure, adrift, or lost. More than ever, we need a sure relationship, a solid foundation, and a secure future.

God's message through his prophets Jeremiah and Hosea is that he is near and that he will be with us when we need him. We can count on God. We can know him. This certainty in our relationship with God enables us to weather the storms around us and to stand firm.

Sip to take away

In a world of change and decline, find your security in God. Come close to him—he is close to you.

a cup of…

Reliance

LIVING WATER

So now, come back to your God! Act on the principles of love and justice, and always live in confident dependence on your God.   HOSEA 12:6

So I tell you, keep on asking, and you will be given what you ask for. Keep on looking, and you will find. Keep on knocking, and the door will be opened. For everyone who asks, receives. Everyone who seeks, finds. And the door is opened to everyone who knocks.   LUKE 11:9-10

When you bow down before the Lord and admit your dependence on him, he will lift you up and give you honor.   JAMES 4:10

Thirst-quenching
thought for the day

As Jesus teaches his disciples about prayer, he
drops in a marvelous nugget of truth: God is always
listening and will respond to our requests and
pleas. Often we get too busy to pray. Sometimes we
become so preoccupied with our problems that we
forget to turn to our heavenly Father. We may feel
as though our needs are small and insignificant
and that God would not be concerned with them.
But Jesus says to persist in our prayers, asking,
seeking, and knocking. God will reward our dependence on him by lifting us up.

The other half of this teaching is just as exciting:
not only is God listening to our prayers, but he will
answer them. If we ask, we will receive. If we seek
answers to our questions, God will reveal them to
us. Of course, God's answers won't always be what
we expect, but as we persist in our reliance on him,
he will respond. God loves us that much.

Sip to take away
Persist in prayer. Talk to your heavenly
Father; he wants to hear from you.

a cup of . . .

Relief

LIVING WATER

Our old sinful selves were crucified with Christ so that sin might lose its power in our lives. We are no longer slaves to sin. ROMANS 6:6

He died for our sins, just as God our Father planned, in order to rescue us from this evil world in which we live. GALATIANS 1:4

I have been crucified with Christ. I myself no longer live, but Christ lives in me. So I live my life in this earthly body by trusting in the Son of God, who loved me and gave himself for me.

GALATIANS 2:19-20

Thirst-quenching thought for the day

It's amazing how prone to sin we are. While we often manage to keep our sinfulness in check in front of others, the truth is that given the opportunity, we often choose to gratify our own desires rather than to obey Christ. Is there any hope for us?

Paul says yes. He acknowledges that we are prone to sin and cannot obey Christ as we should. But he also knows that Christ has provided a new life for us if we are willing to give up our old life. When Jesus was crucified, he died in our place and paid the penalty for our sins. We no longer need to be enslaved to our old way of living or suffer its consequences. That self was crucified with Christ. Now we can live a new life in Christ, allowing him to guide our thoughts and actions. Because we died with Christ, we are forgiven, free, and headed for heaven.

Sip to take away

Jesus loved you so much that he died for you. Now, by faith, you can live for him. You are alive and free. Thank God!

a cup of . . .

Remembrance

LIVING WATER

The women were terrified and bowed low before them. Then the men asked, "Why are you looking in a tomb for someone who is alive? He isn't here! He has risen from the dead! Don't you remember what he told you back in Galilee, that the Son of Man must be betrayed into the hands of sinful men and be crucified, and that he would rise again the third day?" Then they remembered that he had said this.

LUKE 24:5-8

After he was raised from the dead, the disciples remembered that he had said this. And they believed both Jesus and the Scriptures.

JOHN 2:22

Remember what I told you: I am going away, but I will come back to you again.

JOHN 14:28

Thirst-quenching thought for the day

Luke's Gospel records how some of Jesus' followers planned to put spices on Jesus' body. These women knew where he had been buried. But the tomb was empty. Jesus was gone! In his place stood two angels who reminded them of what Jesus had said: he would be crucified but on the third day raised from the dead.

If Jesus' followers had listened and believed in the first place, they would not have expected to find his body in the tomb. But none of them had really understood his prediction; they were surprised by his resurrection! Breathless with excitement, the women rushed back to the eleven disciples with the wonderful news, but the others didn't believe their report.

Do you believe? Christ did rise from the dead! Because of this, we know that God's people are headed for redemption, not disaster. We know that death has been conquered and that we will live forever with Christ. We know that the same power that raised Jesus from the dead is available to help us live for him.

Sip to take away

Do you remember? Do you believe? Then live with joy and hope and power.

a cup of . . .
Renewal

LIVING WATER

Purify me from my sins, and I will be clean; wash me, and I will be whiter than snow.

PSALM 51:7

Create in me a clean heart, O God. Renew a right spirit within me.

PSALM 51:10

I will give you a new heart with new and right desires, and I will put a new spirit in you. I will take out your stony heart of sin and give you a new, obedient heart.

EZEKIEL 36:26

Thirst-quenching
thought for the day

The Bible sometimes uses the image of a cold and hard stone to picture the heart of a person who is closed to God. Hearts become hardened through repeated sin and a life lived for one's self. Sadly, even God's people can become hardened and choose to live their own way rather than to submit to the Lord. Some people seem so hardened, wanting nothing to do with anything remotely spiritual, that we can't imagine anything or anyone breaking through to them. But God can. In fact, he can replace their hearts of stone with new, obedient hearts—soft, alive, warm, and filled with his Spirit.

Sip to take away

Think of a hardened coworker, neighbor, friend, or relative. Ask God to perform spiritual heart surgery on that person . . . and ask him to use you in the process.

a cup of . . .

Rest

LIVING WATER

Now the Lord says, "Stop right where you are! Look for the old, godly way, and walk in it. Travel its path, and you will find rest for your souls."

JEREMIAH 6:16

Jesus said, "Come to me, all of you who are weary and carry heavy burdens, and I will give you rest. Take my yoke upon you. Let me teach you, because I am humble and gentle, and you will find rest for your souls. For my yoke fits perfectly, and the burden I give you is light."

MATTHEW 11:28-30

If you are thirsty, come to me! If you believe in me, come and drink! For the Scriptures declare that rivers of living water will flow out from within.

JOHN 7:37-38

Thirst-quenching
thought for the day

Ad agencies know how to sell. They find a hole and promise to plug it; they find a need and promise to meet it. Then with airbrushed pictures, polished actors, and glib celebrities, they make their pitch . . . guaranteed to satisfy!

Sickened by a steady diet of Madison Avenue, it's easy to build a resistance to such messages. And after dealing with a stream of products that have failed to meet expectations, it's easy to take a cynical look at any new claim.

So, when we hear "Come to me, all of you who are weary . . . and I will give you rest," we may turn away in our minds. Certainly we are weary . . . from carrying heavy responsibilities and working to please God, ourselves, and others. And this claim, like so many others, seems too good to be true. But then we realize who is speaking—Jesus. Jesus tells the truth; he always comes through and lives up to his billing.

Sip to take away

Are you tired of doing it all yourself? Give the burdens that weigh you down to your Lord. Then live refreshed and renewed under his loving kindness and direction.

a cup of . . .

Righteousness

LIVING WATER

Evil people get rich for the moment, but the reward of the godly will last. PROVERBS 11:18

Open up, O heavens, and pour out your righteousness. Let the earth open wide so salvation and righteousness can sprout up together. I, the Lord, created them. ISAIAH 45:8

Plant the good seeds of righteousness, and you will harvest a crop of my love. Plow up the hard ground of your hearts, for now is the time to seek the Lord, that he may come and shower righteousness upon you. HOSEA 10:12

Thirst-quenching
thought for the day

In a garden, the future harvest is directly affected by the choice of seeds and the preparation of the soil. You expect tomatoes, not cucumbers, from tomato seeds. But no seeds will take root and flourish in rock-hard weed-infested soil.

Proverbs 11 points out that godly living yields long-term results—a lasting harvest. Isaiah records God's reminder that both salvation and righteousness ultimately grow from him.

In the passage from Hosea, the prophet expands this great truth and uses it as a spiritual analogy. Those who "plant the good seeds of righteousness" in a willing heart will reap a crop of God's love.

Sip to take away
Do you want to experience God's love? Plow up the hard ground of your heart by confessing your sins and accepting God's forgiveness.

a cup of . . .

Salvation

LIVING WATER

*God saved you by his special favor when you
believed. And you can't take credit for this; it is
a gift from God. Salvation is not a reward for the
good things we have done, so none of us can boast
about it.* EPHESIANS 2:8-9

*God our Savior showed us his kindness and love. He
saved us, not because of the good things we did, but
because of his mercy. He washed away our sins and
gave us a new life through the Holy Spirit. He gener-
ously poured out the Spirit upon us because of what
Jesus Christ our Savior did. He declared us not
guilty because of his great kindness. And now we
know that we will inherit eternal life.* TITUS 3:4-7

Thirst-quenching thought for the day

Often Christians will use the expression "saved" when referring to their relationship with God: "When I was saved . . . ," or "I got saved . . . ," or something similar. That expression comes from passages such as these that refer to God's work for us. When we turn away from our sins and give our lives to Christ, God forgives us and saves us from the penalty we deserve. He also saves us from evil and corruption in the world because we are his children. And he will save us in the future, giving us eternal life when we die.

Is Christ your *Savior?* If so, you are his child, with power for the present and hope for the future.

Sip to take away
Thank God for his love and work on your behalf. Thanks to Christ you can be saved!

a cup of...

Security

LIVING WATER

*The Lord is my shepherd; I have everything I need.
He lets me rest in green meadows; he leads me
beside peaceful streams. He renews my strength. He
guides me along right paths, bringing honor to his
name.*   PSALM 23:1-3

*I am the good shepherd. The good shepherd lays
down his life for the sheep.*   JOHN 10:11

*Once you were wandering like lost sheep. But now
you have turned to your Shepherd, the Guardian of
your souls.*   1 PETER 2:25

Thirst-quenching thought for the day

Put yourself in the mind of a sheep. Enjoy the quiet waters, the green pastures, the cool breezes, the relaxed schedule, the peace of mind. David describes this as a picture of complete contentment. With every need met, the lamb lies still, secure, and safe. But the secret to the lamb's contentment is not the pasture or the stream; it's the loving shepherd, the one who leads, guides, and protects. What a beautiful scene of security.

The apostle Peter learned firsthand the truth of that pastoral picture. And Jesus himself claimed the title of Shepherd.

Today, people desire the lamblike existence described in this psalm. They long for fulfillment, peace, and restoration. In fact, some spend their lifetimes searching for the right formula . . . or seminar . . . or program to achieve that peace. But the secret to contentment is still Jesus, the loving Shepherd.

Sip to take away

Do you want real peace and restoration? Remember the secret: the Shepherd.

a cup of...

Shelter

LIVING WATER

*May the Lord, the God of Israel, under whose wings
you have come to take refuge, reward you fully.*

RUTH 2:12

*Show me your unfailing love in wonderful ways.
You save with your strength those who seek refuge
from their enemies. Guard me as the apple of your
eye. Hide me in the shadow of your wings. Protect
me from wicked people who attack me, from murder-
ous enemies who surround me.*

PSALM 17:7-9

*How precious is your unfailing love, O God! All
humanity finds shelter in the shadow of your
wings.*

PSALM 36:7

Thirst-quenching
thought for the day

David most likely wrote Psalm 17 while being falsely accused and pursued by Saul. David knew that he could call to God, who would hear his prayers and save him from his enemies. David was echoing the sentiments of his great-grandfather Boaz, who acknowledged God's protection over Ruth.

You may not be chased by an army, as David was, but you have probably known people who were against you for some reason or another. Perhaps they spread rumors about you or tried to harm you in other ways. When this happens, remember that God loves you. In fact you, like David and Ruth, are the apple of his eye.

Sip to take away

Regardless of the danger and problems you are encountering, God will watch over you. He will give you refuge in the shadow of his wings.

a cup of . . .

The Lord's Favor

LIVING WATER

Jesus said, "Come to me, all of you who are weary and carry heavy burdens, and I will give you rest. Take my yoke upon you. Let me teach you, because I am humble and gentle, and you will find rest for your souls." MATTHEW 11:28-29

"The Spirit of the Lord is upon me, for he has appointed me to preach Good News to the poor. He has sent me to proclaim that captives will be released, that the blind will see, that the downtrodden will be freed from their oppressors, and that the time of the Lord's favor has come." LUKE 4:18-19

Thirst-quenching thought for the day

Returning to his hometown of Nazareth, Jesus went to the synagogue on the Sabbath day (Luke 4:16). There he stood and read a familiar passage from Isaiah 61:1-2. He explained that the passage referred to him, the promised Messiah, who would deliver God's people.

Most of the people who heard Jesus that day did not understand what he meant; they expected the Messiah to free Israel from Rome. But Jesus meant that he would free poor, imprisoned, blind, and oppressed people from their sins. Jesus did not come to establish a worldly kingdom but to rule in people's hearts.

That's the Good News that people urgently need to see and hear. Jesus is here, and he offers new life to all who will trust in him. To the spiritually impoverished, to those enslaved by their sins, to those blinded by grief, he offers relief and rest. Rejoice and live in this "time of the Lord's favor."

Sip to take away

How can you demonstrate "the Lord's favor" to others who are oppressed and hurting?

a cup of . . .

Trust

LIVING WATER

The Lord is my strength, my shield from every danger. I trust in him with all my heart. He helps me, and my heart is filled with joy. I burst out in songs of thanksgiving.   PSALM 28:7

Jesus shouted to the crowds, "If you trust me, you are really trusting God who sent me."   JOHN 12:44

Don't be troubled. You trust God, now trust in me. There are many rooms in my Father's home, and I am going to prepare a place for you. If this were not so, I would tell you plainly. When everything is ready, I will come and get you, so that you will always be with me where I am.   JOHN 14:1-3

Thirst-quenching
thought for the day

Think of the context of the first verses in John 14. Soon Jesus would die on the cross, rise from the dead, and ascend into heaven. To help prepare the disciples for life without him, Jesus explained that he would be going to his Father, in heaven, and would be preparing a place for them there. He also promised to return.

The disciples were confused—not really believing that he would die, not realizing that he would come back to life, and not understanding at all what he meant by "preparing a place" for them.

But we have the perspective of history. We know that Jesus died on the cross. And we know that he rose from the grave and ascended into heaven. We know he can be trusted to keep his word. Thus we can be confident that he is there *now,* preparing for us.

Sip to take away

What a great promise! If you have trusted in Christ as your Savior, your future is secure—he has a place for you! No one can steal your hope—Jesus is coming back to take you home.

a cup of . . .

Truth

LIVING WATER

God is not a man, that he should lie. He is not a human, that he should change his mind. Has he ever spoken and failed to act? Has he ever promised and not carried it through?   NUMBERS 23:19

This truth gives them the confidence of eternal life, which God promised them before the world began—and he cannot lie.   TITUS 1:2

God has given us both his promise and his oath. These two things are unchangeable because it is impossible for God to lie. Therefore, we who have fled to him for refuge can take new courage, for we can hold on to his promise with confidence.

HEBREWS 6:18

Thirst-quenching
thought for the day

We are surrounded by instability. The winds of change, pressure from peers, temptation, and uncertainty about the future threaten to push us around. We long for a deep foundation, a place to stand, a solid anchor.

We find that in these two "unchangeable" things listed in Hebrews—God's promise and his oath. God is always the same; he never changes. We can count on him to be with us wherever we are and whatever we experience. And we can be certain that God always tells the truth and keeps his promises. God has promised eternal life to all who trust in Christ as Savior.

When you begin to feel pushed this way and that, drop anchor into these truths and take hope. With God, you can weather any storm!

Sip to take away
Use every uncertainty you experience today as a reminder to thank God for his unchanging character and truth.

a cup of . . .
Unconditional Love

LIVING WATER

God so loved the world that he gave his only Son, so that everyone who believes in him will not perish but have eternal life.

JOHN 3:16

God showed his great love for us by sending Christ to die for us while we were still sinners.

ROMANS 5:8

God showed how much he loved us by sending his only Son into the world so that we might have eternal life through him.

1 JOHN 4:9

Thirst-quenching
thought for the day

If you ever feel rejected, abandoned, or unloved, remember the truth of these verses. God loves the world, and he loves you. How do you know? He sent Jesus, his Son, to die in your place and absorb the punishment for your sin. Because of what Jesus has done, you can have new, eternal life by believing in him and accepting him as your personal Savior.

Think of the sacrifice that Jesus made for you. He literally became *sin* on that cross and endured the agony of separation from his Father. You are loved—Jesus proved it!

Sip to take away
As you think about God's unconditional and extravagant love, how does that make you feel? How does it change your perspective on life?

a cup of . . .

Understanding

Living Water

I will call on God, and the Lord will rescue me. Morning, noon, and night I plead aloud in my distress, and the Lord hears my voice.

PSALM 55:16-17

O Lord, I am calling to you. Please hurry! Listen when I cry to you for help!   PSALM 141:1

This High Priest of ours understands our weaknesses, for he faced all of the same temptations we do, yet he did not sin. So let us come boldly to the throne of our gracious God. There we will receive his mercy, and we will find grace to help us when we need it.   HEBREWS 4:15-16

Thirst-quenching
thought for the day

David probably wrote Psalm 55 during the time of his son Absalom's rebellion and his advisor Ahithophel's treachery (2 Samuel 15–18). During his exile, David must have felt devastated, having been abandoned by his son and his close friend. He cried out to God in his grief, anger, and confusion. David was confident that God would hear his prayer, give him courage and strength, and save him from his enemies.

That cry of David's was no isolated act of desperation. It was a habit. Even when his troubles were of his own making, David never hesitated to turn to God. He trusted fully in God's understanding and grace.

Our own reliance on God flows from an even clearer reason. Hebrews 4 tells us that Jesus really does understand, by experience, what we go through. We can "come boldly" to him for help!

Sip to take away
Are you feeling overwhelmed?
surrounded by enemies? abandoned? Call
on the Lord for his peace and his power.
He understands you!

a cup of . . .

Unfailing love

LIVING WATER

He passed in front of Moses and said, "I am the Lord, I am the Lord, the merciful and gracious God. I am slow to anger and rich in unfailing love and faithfulness."   EXODUS 34:6

The Lord is like a father to his children, tender and compassionate to those who fear him.

PSALM 103:13

The Lord is kind and merciful, slow to get angry, full of unfailing love. The Lord is good to everyone. He showers compassion on all his creation.

PSALM 145:8-9

Thirst-quenching thought for the day

What experiences does the word *compassion* conjure up for you? Remember falling off your tricycle and skinning your knee? Your mother didn't accuse you of being clumsy; she held you close, wiped away your tears, and bandaged your knee. She taught you compassion.

Remember as a teenager when you came home hours after curfew and found your parents waiting? Although you didn't like the punishment, you knew that your parents cared about you. Good parents love their children and are "tender and compassionate" with them.

That's the way David describes our heavenly Father: "slow to get angry, full of unfailing love." God wants only what is best for us. When we fall, he dries our tears and puts us back on our feet again. When we sin, he hears our cries and forgives. God shows us unfailing love.

Sip to take away

When you've fallen or fallen away, go home. Your Father awaits you with open arms.

a cup of...

Victorious Peace

LIVING WATER

"I have told you all this so that you may have peace in me. Here on earth you will have many trials and sorrows. But take heart, because I have overcome the world."

JOHN 16:33

Never pay back evil for evil to anyone. Do things in such a way that everyone can see you are honorable. Do your part to live in peace with everyone, as much as possible.

ROMANS 12:17-18

Every child of God defeats this evil world by trusting Christ to give the victory. And the ones who win this battle against the world are the ones who believe that Jesus is the Son of God.

1 JOHN 5:4-5

Thirst-quenching thought for the day

Jesus was about to be arrested, tried, and crucified. Soon his disciples would be left behind to carry his message throughout the world. Jesus knew that they would be persecuted, so in his final instructions (John 16) he warned them and gave them a promise.

Note that Jesus didn't say the disciples "might" or "could" have trouble. He said they "will." Yet in their trials they could have peace and be encouraged.

Until Christ returns, Christians will always be in conflict with the world. We stand out. We have a different allegiance, one with different values and a different lifestyle. We threaten the status quo by refusing to compromise our faith. We live for Christ and call people to turn from their sins and to give their lives to the Savior. That certainly won't make us popular. We will have trouble.

Despite all this, we can have peace. Knowing that our Lord has defeated sin and death, we are given courage in the face of trials and God's peace amidst our sorrows.

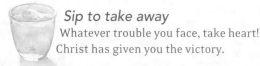

Sip to take away

Whatever trouble you face, take heart! Christ has given you the victory.

a cup of . . .
Weakness

LIVING WATER

In everything we do we try to show that we are true ministers of God. We patiently endure troubles and hardships and calamities of every kind.

2 CORINTHIANS 6:4

Each time he said, "My gracious favor is all you need. My power works best in your weakness." So now I am glad to boast about my weaknesses, so that the power of Christ may work through me. Since I know it is all for Christ's good, I am quite content with my weaknesses and with insults, hardships, persecutions, and calamities. For when I am weak, then I am strong. 2 CORINTHIANS 12:9-10

Although he died on the cross in weakness, he now lives by the mighty power of God. We, too, are weak, but we live in him and have God's power—the power we use in dealing with you. 2 CORINTHIANS 13:4

Thirst-quenching thought for the day

In a world that believes in "survival of the fittest," we are told that we must be hard, tough, and strong in order to succeed. But God's way is different. He wants us to be humble and vulnerable before him. He promises to use our weaknesses for his glory. When Paul wrote to the Corinthian believers, he challenged them with his own vulnerability. He revealed how much he struggled with a thorn in his flesh (see 2 Corinthians 12:7) and "insults, hardships, persecutions, and calamities." Rather than allowing his struggles and problems to defeat him, Paul found his strength in Christ's power, which allowed him to be content in his weakness. God wants us to discover the same source of strength.

Sip to take away

Where are you weak? Rejoice! People will be drawn to Christ when they see his power working in you, making you strong. God can use your limitations and problems.

a cup of . . .

Wisdom

LIVING WATER

*By wisdom the Lord founded the earth; by under-
standing he established the heavens.*

PROVERBS 3:19

*Oh, what a wonderful God we have! How great are
his riches and wisdom and knowledge! How impossible it is for us to understand his decisions and his
methods! For who can know what the Lord is thinking? Who knows enough to be his counselor? And
who could ever give him so much that he would have
to pay it back? For everything comes from him;
everything exists by his power and is intended for
his glory. To him be glory evermore. Amen.*

ROMANS 11:33-36

Thirst-quenching thought for the day

In the last few chapters of his letter to the Romans, Paul discusses God's sovereign plan for both Jews and Gentiles in great detail. In Romans 11, Paul breaks into praise for who God is and for the wisdom of his plan. Paul's praise echoes the experiences of countless others to whom God has allowed a glimpse of his character and plans.

Although God's methods are beyond our comprehension, we know that he governs the universe and our lives in perfect wisdom, justice, and love. No one has fully understood the mind of the Lord; God alone possess absolute power and wisdom. In the final analysis, all of us are absolutely dependent on him. He sustains and rules our world, and he works out all things to bring glory to himself. The all-powerful God deserves our gratitude and adoration.

Sip to take away

Consider what God has done in your life and how his wise plans have worked out for the best. Praise his holy name!

a cup of...

Wonder

LIVING WATER

When I look at the night sky and see the work of your fingers—the moon and the stars you have set in place—what are mortals that you should think of us, mere humans that you should care for us?

PSALM 8:3-4

The heavens tell of the glory of God. The skies display his marvelous craftsmanship. Day after day they continue to speak; night after night they make him known.

PSALM 19:1-2

He said to God, "I will declare the wonder of your name to my brothers and sisters. I will praise you among all your people."

HEBREWS 2:12

Thirst-quenching thought for the day

Meeting God certainly has a pulse-quickening effect. Do you want a glimpse of what God is like? Look at the skies—the whirling galaxies, the sparkling stars, the shiny planets all choreographed as one—and see his glory. Who can say there is no God, no evidence for his existence? All one has to do is look and listen. Opportunities for wonder surround us every moment.

David expressed a continual state of wonder over God's craftsmanship evident throughout his creation. But even more glorious than that is the fact that this awesome God is interested in us—his tiny, finite creatures. The Creator loves us, and we are wonderfully gifted with the capacity to love him back.

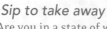

Sip to take away

Are you in a state of wonder? Whenever you need a refreshing dose of God's might and power, look at the night sky.

a cup of . . .

Worry-Free Living

LIVING WATER

Take delight in the Lord, and he will give you your heart's desires.

PSALM 37:4

Trust in the Lord with all your heart; do not depend on your own understanding. Seek his will in all you do, and he will direct your paths.

PROVERBS 3:5-6

Your heavenly Father already knows all your needs, and he will give you all you need from day to day if you live for him and make the Kingdom of God your primary concern. So don't worry about tomorrow, for tomorrow will bring its own worries. Today's trouble is enough for today.

MATTHEW 6:32-34

Thirst-quenching thought for the day

Worry is sickening. Anxiety is epidemic. People worry about what they have and what they don't have, about the past and the future. Instead of being anxious, Jesus tells us to turn our lives over to God. If we put him at the center of our lives, he will give us everything we need. We have no need to worry.

What thoughts keep you awake at night? a relationship? money? your career? Perhaps you worry because that person or possession holds the place of highest importance for you. Reserve that spot for Christ, and let him reorder your life. Then take a deep breath and relax.

Sip to take away

In what areas of your life do you need to trust the Lord to guide your paths?

Subject Index

Scripture Index